THE ULTIMATE SALE

A FINANCIALLY SIMPLE GUIDE TO SELLING A BUSINESS FOR MAXIMUM PROFIT

JUSTIN A. GOODBREAD

CFP®, CEPA®, CVGA®

ISBN: 978-1-7320599-0-0 (print)
ISBN: 978-1-7320599-2-4 (ebook)

Ordering Information:
Special discounts are available on quantity purchases by corporations, associations, and others. For details, contact email info@financiallysimple.com.

To Emily, the love of my life.

DISCLOSURE

CONTENTS

PHASE 2: SELL YOUR BUSINESS FOR PROFIT

Get Yourself Ready for the Sale

List Your Business for Sale

Negotiate the Sale

Close the Sale

PREFACE

I didn't begin my financial career in the traditional sense. I didn't graduate from a public high school, go straight to a four-year college, leave with a finance degree, join a firm, and move my way up through the ranks. That's not who I am.

I'm just an ole country boy from the small town of Brunswick, Georgia. I grew up on the ocean, running around barefoot and chasing alligators in the smelly air. I was homeschooled, so I had the opportunity to learn and complete classes at my own (quick) pace. That independence led me to start my first business cutting lawns when I was just 15 years old to keep busy and to work outside with my hands on the land that I loved.

After high school, I went to Abraham Baldwin Agricultural College and graduated with a degree in horticulture. My dream was to build "Lawn Care by the Boys" into the world's greatest landscaping company where I could do everything from cutting grass to designing complex hardscapes.

The direction of my life changed at that time when I met Emily, the love of my life, and got married. We decided to move to the "big city" of Knoxville to be close to her family. I sold the landscaping business I had down in Brunswick, took the profit I earned, and came to Tennessee.

Some years later, a friend of mine recruited me into the world of finance by offering me a $5,000 sign-on bonus if I could pass three exams. He didn't think I could pass the test with only 30 days to study, but I sure did! A week after I passed the tests, corporate shut down the local office that hired me. I wasn't sure what I wanted to do from there, but I knew for sure what I didn't want to do. I didn't want to trade stocks because I saw it as a constant gamble. I also didn't want to sell insurance because I would go broke if I had to depend on my sales skills. Although I love speaking in front of groups of people and talking to people one-on-one, I don't enjoy mixers where I have to sell a name and a product.

1

What I did instead was become a CFP® in 2006 and pursue a business degree from the University of Phoenix®. Since I could set my own pace through its online program, I graduated with my bachelor's degree in a year and a half while working as a partner in a financial firm and becoming a dad for the second time.

As I gained more and more experience in the world of business and financial planning, I realized that I had a knack and a passion for helping fellow small business owners. I loved breaking complex financial concepts into *Financially Simple* terms. That led me to earn the CEPA (Certified Exit Planning Advisor) and the CVGA® (Certified Value Growth Advisor) designations. I would use my skills to guide business owners through value growth, sales, mergers, or buyouts, and ultimately prepare them for the next chapter in their lives: retirement.

I've started five companies within my 25 years in business beginning at age 15. All companies were profitable and in the black in revenue. I've personally sold three of those businesses *for profit* and still run the other two successfully.

My broad realm of experiences in business led me to start "Financially Simple," a financial blog, podcast, and video education portal that tries to make finances *simple* for small business owners. My work within "Financially Simple" has catapulted me into the national press. I currently write for *Kiplinger* and *Forbes*. My name has appeared in many national media venues and in a litany of written publications. I am regularly asked to speak about business at national conventions, trade associations, and business events around the nation.

I've earned local acclaim and national recognition because I understand business and more importantly, I understand how personal financial planning and business planning integrate. I get it. Not many people do.

Ultimately, I've written this book to show you, the business owner, how to create value and accelerate growth in your company to sell the business for top dollar within ten years' time. According to the Small Business Administration, half of small businesses fail within five years, and 69 percent of the other half will fail within ten years[1]. I don't want you to become a statistic.

---

1   U.S. Small Business Administration Office of Advocacy. (2017, August). *Frequently Asked Question about Small Businesses* [Report]. Retrieved from the SBA website: https://www.sba.gov/sites/default/files/advocacy/SB-FAQ-2017-WEB.pdf

I want to help *you* create, direct, and fulfill your business visions. You may have no intention of selling your business anytime soon, but many of my clients say that they want to work hard for ten years and then get out of business; they tell me that their business goal is "10 and Sold."

Even if you do not plan on selling your business in ten years, you can begin increasing its value to make it sellable for profit by that time. For the purposes of this book, we will set our sale sights on a ten-year timeline. Let's start working toward your Ultimate Sale!

WHY THIS BOOK MATTERS

Too many business owners walk away from their businesses
without realizing profit.

BUSINESS EXIT STATISTICS ARE STARTLING

Corporate America can be divided into three segments: The micro market, the lower middle market, and the upper middle market. Traditionally, businesses that gross under $5 million in sales fall into the micro market. Businesses that receive between $5 million and $100 million in revenue each year represent the lower middle market, and companies that earn $100 million or more make up the upper middle market and above.

According to statistics compiled by the US Census Bureau in 2015, roughly 93 percent of businesses in the United States are part of the micro market, and these 5.6 million "small business" ventures hire approximately 34 million employees.[2]

By contrast, about 6 percent of businesses in the U.S. fall into the lower middle market arena; yet those "mid-size" companies employ around 30 million employees. Thus, while mid-size companies only hold 6 percent of the market share, they employ 25 percent of the North American workforce. To put that in perspective, realize that small businesses (those companies with less

---

2   United States Census Bureau. (2015). 2015 SUSB Annual Data Tables by Establishment Industry. Retrieved from https://www.census.gov/data/tables/2015/econ/susb/2015-susb-annual.html

than 500 employees) hold almost 94 percent of the market share, but they only employ 29 percent of America's workforce.[3]

Why is that? If micro business owners represent about 94 percent of businesses in existence, why do they employ almost the same amount of people mid-size businesses employ? Well, many small business owners are sole proprietors or single owners working for themselves. These stand-alone, do-it-yourself business owners have a business, but they have no employees. These practitioners are often your artisans, handymen, and the like who can operate from their homes or out of the trunk of their cars.

Whereas when you get into that lower middle market where businesses gross between $5 million and $10 million, owners need teams and employees in place to handle that higher level of production, sales, or service. However, that lower middle market only represents 351,000 businesses of the six million or so in existence in the US. I think that's interesting.

Although the lower middle market may not hold a majority share of businesses in corporate America, they do gross $5.8 trillion of sales, or 20 percent of market sales, while small businesses gross roughly $3.5 trillion in revenue, making up 12 percent of the total market sales. If you do the math, that means that the large-sized companies—the big businesses—are crushing sales at $20.3 trillion, or 68 percent of total sales in the United States.[4]

3   Beesley, Caryn. U.S. Small Business Association. (July 21, 2016). How and Why to Determine if Your Business is Small. Retrieved from https://www.sba.gov/blogs/how-and-why-determine-if-your-business-small

4   Corporate Value Metrics. (2013). U.S. Market Segments. https://www.corporatevalue.net/

U.S. Market Segments

	Sales Range	#of Cos (thousands)	%	Sales $ (trillions)	%	# of EEs (thousands)	%
Micro Market	<$5M	5,678	93.9%	3.57	12%	34,764	29%
Lower Middle Market	$5M - $100M	351	5.8%	5.84	20%	29,712	25%
Upper Mid Mkt and Above	>$100M	21	0.3%	20.33	68%	56,128	47%
Total Employer Firms		6,050	100%	29.74	100%	120,604	100%
Non-Employer Firms		21,708		0.99			
Total All Firms		**27,758**		**30.73**			

Data used by permission of Corporate Value Metrics. www.CorporateValue.net

In another private market study updated yearly, Pepperdine University concurred that approximately 351,000 businesses in the United States earn between $5 million and $100 million. Researchers involved in this *Pepperdine Private Capital Markets Report* went on to say that out of these 351,000 mid-size businesses, about 250,000 of business owners are expected to try to exit their businesses by the year 2030. That's almost three quarters of the middle market businesses. That could potentially affect the majority of the 25 percent of American employees within the mid-market, or 21 million people! If this is the year 2019, and we're looking forward to the year 2030, then we're looking at three quarters of mid-sized businesses trying to sell in 11 years' time.

But why? Why are so many business owners looking to sell their current businesses by 2030? Baby Boomers who would normally be retiring in stages over the last several years suffered through the economic recession that began around 2007. Those individuals who thought they would be selling lost many of their assets during the recession, and they are looking at about another 10 years to recoup enough of their assets to sell their companies. If that many business owners are trying to sell at the same time, what are your chances of selling your business?

Now here's where it gets scary. Of those 250,000 mid-size companies that will try to sell within the next 11 years, only roughly 25,000 will be deemed market ready to sell according to the AM&AA. Then of those 25,000 deemed market-ready, only 15,000 will sell.[5] *That's a 40 percent transaction failure rate from that 25,000 who are "ready" to sell! If you think about it long enough, you'll realize that 94 percent of the 250,000 who wanted to sell in the first place will not sell. That's 235,000 business owners whose dreams will not come true. How scary is that?*

Of those 15,000 business owners who do sell their companies, just over 50 percent of them will have to sell with concessions. In other words, they will have to reduce their sales price, offer seller-carried notes, offer stock options, or the like to get the deal finalized. So essentially, 7,500 of the 15,000 business owners who sell their companies will not get what they want. That leaves roughly 7,500 mid-size business owners who will sell at their desired value.

Let's put all of that into perspective. *There are currently 351,000 business owners in the middle market, and of those who want to sell in the next 11 years (about 250,000), 3 percent will sell for listing price.* Ouch. I don't know about you but that's depressing to me, and we're only talking about those who sell in the mid-market.

According to the Exit Planning Institute (EPI), 80 percent of companies below $50 million in revenue never sell. 80 percent. That's not even talking about owners who want to sell within the next 10 years. That's talking about 80 percent of ALL small businesses, or 4.5 million companies! That is crazy! Another statistic from the EPI tells us that only 30 percent of family businesses survive into the second generation. Do you understand that? There is only a 30 percent chance that I will pass my business down to my children. If I don't pass it down to my children or sell it, what will happen to it? Well, if statistics are correct, most will close without sale or fanfare.

Why are business exit numbers so dismal? What is happening between a company's beginning and its end to make it unsellable? Why are your chances of selling your business and selling it for what you want virtually impossible? I see a possible answer when I read the EPI's report that *only 25 percent of*

5   Alliance of Merger & Acquisition Advisors. (n.d.) Expanding the Conversation: Middle Market Value Growth. Retrieved from https://www.amaaonline.com/value-growth/.

business owners have a basic financial plan. Only 25 percent. That is pathetic to me because business owners are some of the brightest people I know. If they're going to spend their entire lives and time working in their business, why wouldn't they take care of it by planning for its financial success?

And the problem is compounded because 80 percent of business owners' net worth is tied up in their business.

Stop and think about that for a second. If you are a business owner, statistics say that 80 percent of your net worth is tied up in an asset that is only 12 percent likely to sell at its end. That is like having a dividend stock or CD that provides you with an adequate income, but you never own the actual asset. The asset is not worth anything other than the monthly dividend earned from it. Even worse than that, you are fighting, striving, shedding blood, and working long hours just to earn that monthly income. Yet, that is where 80 percent of our business owners are today.[6]

WE CAN RISE ABOVE STATISTICS

If we can understand what led to the success of the 12 percent of business owners who sold their companies, we can model our business after theirs to do the same thing, *and* we can do it on our own timeline.

---

6   U.S. Small Business Administration Office of Advocacy. (2017, August). *Frequently Asked Question about Small Businesses* [Report]. Retrieved from the SBA website: https://www.sba. gov/sites/default/files/advocacy/SB-FAQ-2017-WEB.pdf

PREPARE YOUR BUSINESS FOR SALE

"Companies that solely focus on competition will ultimately die. Those that focus on value creation will thrive."

Edward de Bono

Decide to Sell

"There is no sale without the story; no knockout without the setup."

Gary Vaynerchuk

Whether you have been in business one year or 20 years, make the decision to sell your business. Don't leave its eventual end to chance. Plan and dictate how you want to leave so that you can walk away profitable rather than walk away bereft.

CHAPTER 1

MAKE A DECISION TO SELL

"Unsuccessful people make decisions based on their current situations.
Successful people make decisions based on where they want to be."

Unknown

SELLING A HOUSE

If you own your home and decide to sell it, chances are you already have a sales price in mind and a vision of the money you will make upon its sale. You know how much you owe on your mortgage, and you know how much money you need to make to put a down payment on a new house, to pay off debts on credit cards or cars, to take a dream vacation, or to do any number of things you have a mind to do.

Likewise, you probably have a vision in mind of where you will live next. Will you move in with family while you build a house? Will you downsize to a small house since the kids are all grown up and out of the house? Are you moving to a condominium or apartment complex so that you do not have to maintain a yard anymore? Are you transitioning into an assisted living facility? Generally speaking, people do not sell their homes without knowing where they will live next.

Upon deciding to sell your house and deciding what you will do after its sale, you begin preparing for the sale. Most likely, you will not just stick a "For Sale" sign in your yard and hope for the best. No friends, if you want to sell a house and sell it for the most amount of money possible, you follow a fairly standard process.

Assuming you do not want to list the house yourself, you would most likely contact a REALTOR® who has connections with local appraisers and home inspectors. Altogether, you would examine your house's foundation for structural issues, its nooks and crannies for hidden problems, and its general appearance for aesthetic appeal. Your team would also assess your house's style (i.e. Rancher, Colonial, Shotgun, Detached, Attached, Condominium, Tri-Level, etc.), room count, square footage, improvements, and condition. By analyzing all the information your team's assessment provides, you can determine your home's intrinsic value.

Next, you and your team would research comparable homes that have sold recently within your neighborhood or within a nearby radius. What were their final sales prices? Do they match your home's determined base value? Did they sell for more money or less money than that value? What made those houses different than yours? Did they have amenities yours does not have? Does your house have amenities theirs did not? Does your interior design style reflect the fashions of the 1970s, while your neighbors' houses have modern design features? Would you need to make updates to your house to sell it for a comparable price? Could you sell it for more?

After a thorough analysis of your home's assets and its condition compared to the homes that sold around it, your team can calculate your house's current fair market value, which could be above or below its intrinsic value. At this point in time, you have a decision to make. Do you want to list your house for sale at its current market value, or would you like to increase its value before you sell it? If you are happy with the assessed price, then you are ready! You would sign a contract with your REALTOR® and put your house on the market.

However, if you are not satisfied with the money you would likely make from your house's sale, you must do something to change its current condition. Maybe you need to paint walls or replace carpets. Perhaps you need to gut a bathroom or redo your kitchen. Should you lay new floors or pressure wash your vinyl siding? Do you need to replace your roof or clean your gutters? Will your home improvements take a couple of weeks or a period of months? Should you hire a contractor to guide your renovation projects, or will you attempt them all yourself? Do you have to stay within a certain budget? Will that limit your grand design and ambitions?

Ultimately, what must you do to increase your home's sellable value from "X" to "Y"? Whether you need to make small changes or embark upon major renovations, you must begin with an end in mind. How can you plan improvements if you do not have an end valuation in mind?

SELLING A BUSINESS

Selling a business should be no different than selling a house. Long before you sign sales documents at a closing table, you make a decision to sell. Most likely, you have already envisioned what that sale looks like. Do you want to pass your business down to future generations or to key employees? Would you like to sell your business on the open marketplace to a business buyer or to a strategic competitor? How much money do you want to take away from the sale? What amount will allow you to reach your personal and workplace goals?

If you decide to pass a tangible asset and professional career down to the next generation, you will begin your sales process differently than if you want to sell a booming business for maximum profit in the big business market. Whether you want to make enough money to send your kids to college without taking out loans or you want to live a life of leisure off the earnings from your business sale, you have a vision of what you want the money you make from the sale of your business to do for you.

Assuming you will not try to sell the business on your own, you would then seek help and advice from knowledgeable financial, tax, legal, and business advisors. With all your advisors working with you, you would examine your entity choice, your business's operations, your assets, your historic financial growth, your current financial status, and your future financial forecast for structural soundness. Upon evaluating every aspect of your business, your advisory team could determine your company's fundamental, intrinsic value.

Next, you and your team would research comparable companies within your market—small business, mid-market, or big business. Have any comparable businesses been able to sell? What were their purchase prices? Is that price above or below your intrinsic value? Is there a gap in the value of the comparable company and your company? Why? What makes the comparable companies different than yours? Does anything set your business apart from theirs?

After a thorough analysis of your business's current structure and comparable companies, your team can calculate your business's value. Like selling a house, you now have a decision to make. Do you want to list your business for sale at its current value, or would you like to increase its value before you sell it? Does your business's actual value match your envisioned value? If you are happy with the determined price and will have enough money to accomplish your goals and fulfill your visions, then go ahead! Find a transition expert, and put your business up for sale.

However, if you are not satisfied with the money you could make now from your business's sale or you need more money than the sale would yield you at this point in time to accomplish your retirement or lifetime goals, then *you must do something to decrease the gap between what you will earn versus what you need to earn.* In other words, you must increase your business's value to earn what you need from its sale in the future.

Maybe you need to incorporate better operational systems or employee training methods. Perhaps you need to increase your profit margins or production turnaround times. Can you incentivize employees to increase sales or service? Could you do a better job marketing or advertising? How does your management team function, and can it do a better job? Can you mass produce a current product?

Ultimately, once you identify your areas of weakness, or low value, you and your advisory team can make a plan to strengthen those areas and increase your company's value from "X" to "Y," but you have to know "Y's" value. Whether you need to make small, quick changes, or embark upon years of structural improvements, you must begin the sales process with the end goal in mind. Knowing the price you need upon the sale of your business will direct your decisions while you are getting your business ready to sell. It will help you prioritize changes and improvements, and provide you with ideas on how to make those changes. Then, once you reach your ideal market value—quickly or 10 years from now—you can sell!

While I cannot give anyone guidance on selling a house, I can offer fellow small business owners some sound information to guide them through the sale of their companies. *Ultimately, my purpose for writing this book is to help business owners get the full value they need from the sale of their business to accomplish their future business and personal goals.*

CHAPTER 2

ASSEMBLE YOUR ADVISORY TEAM

*"Great things in business are never done by one person.
They're done by a team of people."*

Steve Jobs

THE ORIGINAL "DREAM TEAM"

If you are over the age of 35, more than likely the term "Dream Team" conjures up memories of Larry Bird running down the court alongside Magic Johnson as he throws an alley-oop to Michael Jordan. Back in 1992, Olympics' officials changed rules to allow professional players to compete in the games, and the NBA (the National Basketball Association) handpicked a team to compete for the USA on the basketball court. Essentially, NBA executives chose the players they thought were the best of the best at that time, assembling a "Dream Team" whose skill sets allowed them to stomp the competition and take home the gold medal.

On this Dream Team, players Larry Bird, Magic Johnson, Michael Jordan, Charles Barkley, Karl Malone, Clyde Drexler, John Stockton, Scottie Pippen, Chris Mullin, David Robinson, Patrick Ewing, and Christian Laettner more than dominated the competition and attracted crowds wherever they went. Head coach, Chuck Daly, once said that "Travelling with the Dream Team was like travelling with 12 rock stars."[7] Even opponents set aside team loyalties to snap photos of themselves standing next to these players or playing against them. Daly reflected on that phenomenon by saying, "[Competing players]

---

7   NBA's Greatest Moments: The Original Dream Team. (n.d.). Retrieved from http://www. nba.com/history/dreamT_moments.html

knew they were playing the world's best. In fact, they could go home the rest of their lives and tell their kids, 'I played against Michael Jordan and Magic Johnson and Larry Bird.'"[8]

YOUR BUSINESS'S DREAM TEAM[9]

Once you decide to sell a business, friends, you need to assemble the same kind of Dream Team. Not one person can sell a business by himself. No, you need a team of players who can listen to your ideas, challenge you, correct you, refocus you, direct you, mentor you, balance you, and help you. You need these team members to evaluate your business for sale worthiness, determine what steps you need to take to increase your business's value if necessary, walk with you as you add value to your existing business, and guide you as you list and sell your business. If you want your company's sales price to compare to the price of the best of the best in your marketplace, you need to build a Dream Team of professional advisors who know how to make that happen. In that case, who are these advisors? Which professionals can best guide you through your business's sale process?

The CFP®

To me, one of the most important players on your sales team is a CERTIFIED FINANCIAL PLANNER™. Referred to as a CFP®, these professionals often have varying licenses in real estate, insurance, mortgages, business acquisitions, business sales, or stocks and bonds. However, you are looking for a CFP® who specializes in business planning or business exit planning to act as the captain of your team.

Now is not the time to enlist the help of the average financial advisor who works for the Wall Street firms. These advisors typically work solely with investment accounts and investment options. In other words, they work in market

8   NBA's Greatest Moments: The Original Dream Team. (n.d.). Retrieved from http://www.nba.com/history/dreamT_moments.html
9   For more information on this topic, refer to https://financiallysimple.com/essential-professional-advisory-team-members-for-a-startup/

securities, not in business advising. Sure, as you prepare to sell your business, you will need someone to manage your investments, but you need so much more than that. You need business planning, tax planning, investment planning, wealth management planning, budget planning, legal advice, employee advice, management advice, value growth advice, and more. Traditional CFPs® work as stock brokers, earning commissions and fees from selling investment products to individuals, and those employed in that capacity will most likely be of no use to you in a business sale.

Instead, find a multi-credentialed CFP® who can guide you through preparations for your business sale, through the closing of the sale, and through your life after the sale. A CFP® who has a Certified Exit Planning Advisor (CEPA) certification and a Certified Value Growth Advisor (CVGA®) certification can offer you sound *guidance* throughout every stage of your business's sale and throughout every stage of your personal financial life. When you look for the right individual to captain your exit team, be sure to look for one who can handle this multifaceted type of long-term relationship and for one who works independently of Wall Street's investment expectations.

Additionally, as you look for a financial advisor to fill this role on your team, make sure you find one who has the actual CFP® designation. You see, the CFP® Board requires its members to abide by certain practice standards and codes of conduct to remain certified. For example, a CFP® must lay out in writing exactly what he plans to do for his client and what fees he intends to charge for that scope of engagement. Additionally, the board requires its certified members to be fiduciaries or professionals who use their knowledge, education, and experience to act in your best interest.[10] In my financially simple terms, as a fiduciary, the CERTIFIED FINANCIAL PLANNER™ makes financial decisions on your behalf as if he were in your shoes.

The CPA

The next team member you want to hire right off the bat to prepare your business for sale is a Certified Public Accountant. Referred to as a CPA, I like

10 United States Department of Labor. Fiduciary Responsibilities. (n.d.) Retrieved from https://www.dol.gov/general/topic/retirement/fiduciaryresp

to call this advisor the point guard of your Dream Team. This professional typically crunches numbers, prepares financial reports, strategizes how to minimize tax liabilities, and audits books for business compliance with the Securities & Exchange Commission. Like a CERTIFIED FINANCIAL PLANNER™, a CPA must abide by certain ethical standards and codes of conduct required and enforced by a Certified Accounting Board, so you will not be dealing with a salesperson who is just trying to sell you a product. Unlike the CFP®, your CPA will be involved in measuring, disclosing, and providing financial information you need to prepare your business for its sale and to sell it.

The Attorney

Next, you need a burly team member who can block shots from business buyers and get rebounds during purchase negotiations. Essentially, an attorney fills the role of center on your Dream Team. Now whenever I say "attorney," I am not talking about a litigator or an injury lawyer. I am talking about a business attorney who can help you understand the law in regard to your business dealings and your business sale. You need a professional who can help you understand business contracts, who can write sales contracts and purchase agreements, who can act in due diligence for you and with you, and who can work with you on estate planning upon the close of your business.

THREE PLAYERS MAKE ONE INCREDIBLE TEAM

To me, those three advisors—your CFP®, your CPA, and your attorney—are the core players on your Dream Team, and they will guide you through the business sale process. You have your tax, your legal, and your planning fields all wrapped up together, each professional looking at a business's valuation, growth, and sale in a unique way. However, each field overlaps a little bit. A CFP knows some information about taxes and law, but he does not practice tax or law. CPAs and attorneys know planning, but they do not practice planning. If you can get each one working together, you could end up with a true "Dream Team."

CHAPTER 3

PLAN FOR THE FUTURE

"Whether you are just entering the workforce or nearing retirement age, planning for the future is critical."

Ron Lewis

B efore you begin assessing your business's worth and sellability with your "Dream Team," you need to evaluate your personal financial stability with those advisors. If you spend all your time investing in your business and none of your time investing outside of your business, then what happens if you never sell?

A fulfilling and happy retirement means different things to different people. For some, it may be a period of transition from full-time business ownership to full-time or part-time employment. For others, it may mean spending more time with family and loved ones. Still others envision doing more of what they love to do in retirement like golfing, gardening, fishing, or crafting. Once you decide how you want to spend your time and energy in retirement, it's time to start building a personal retirement plan.

#1 - DEFINE YOUR RETIREMENT

First, you want to define what retirement looks like to you. Create goals for this time in your life, and write down your objectives. In the beginning, focus on your hopes and dreams rather than on your budget, and be as specific as you can. For instance, instead of saying you want to "travel more" in retirement, write down that you want to do something like "tour German castles," "go on an Alaskan cruise," or maybe even "see the Northern Lights." Rather than saying you want to "see family more often," write down that you'd like to "take your children and grandchildren to Disney World." Instead of saying you want to "fish more often," write down that you'd like to "fish twice a week."

After you have compiled an extensive list of retirement goals and objectives, start eliminating objectives that would create financial burdens on you or your family. Be real and practical about what you can or can't do physically and financially during retirement. The more realistic you are, the more tangible your goals will be. Eventually, limit your list to your top five to 10 attainable retirement goals. Those remaining objectives will be the start of your retirement visions.

#2 - TAKE A LOOK AT YOUR INVESTMENTS

If you are like most business owners I know, you haven't saved much outside of your business for retirement. You are hoping that your business's sale will be your big lottery ticket into retirement. However, if you've made a decision to sell your business within a certain period of time, now is the time to start saving as much as possible in retirement accounts, savings accounts, and the like.

Talk to your financial planner about your current investments or about making new investments. Do you need to take minimum, moderate, or maximum risks within your investment portfolios? Do you need to diversify your assets within your retirement accounts? Should you contribute the maximum amount possible to your accounts each year? While you are planning to grow the value of your company, plan to grow the value of your personal assets, too.

#3 - EVALUATE YOUR HEALTH

If you are making goals and setting aside money to prepare for retirement, then reaching retirement healthy will be vital for you to experience the luxuries you're planning. From ordinary physicals to biannual teeth cleanings, a little preventative medical attention or a few doctors' visits can go a long way toward keeping you healthy.

Work with your doctor or health provider to maintain or improve your health. Commit or recommit yourself to eating healthy foods, exercising, and getting enough sleep. Stay mentally acute with brain teasers and puzzles, and stay emotionally healthy by maintaining contact with friends and family members.

#4 - DETERMINE WHEN TO COLLECT SOCIAL SECURITY

Like most people in the United States, part of your retirement monies will probably come through a monthly stipend from the Social Security Administration. How much you will receive in monthly benefits during your retirement years is determined by the amount you've contributed to Social Security during your working years and by the age you start collecting Social Security.

The longer you wait to claim Social Security benefits, the greater the benefits are for you and your family. Whether you are single, married, divorced, or widowed, it usually pays to be patient to claim. If you are not sure how much you have contributed, how much you will receive monthly, or when you should claim your benefits, talk to your financial advisors or look through the government's Social Security website (www.ssa.gov).

#5 - CREATE A RETIREMENT BUDGET[11]

While you are assessing how much money you will need to retire, it is important to make a list of your current assets, your current debts, your current income, and your current expenses. Essentially, you want to see how much it costs you to live now and how much it will cost you to live the life of your dreams during your retirement years.

Start by tracking your income and expenses for a couple of months. Then, prepare a formal budget that ensures your income exceeds your expenses each month. If you have extra money, do you need to start paying down debts or

11 Visit https://financiallysimple.com/personal-budget for a personal budget template.

saving more in your retirement accounts? Do you need to change your lifestyle and cut your expenses before retirement to guarantee you'll have enough money for retirement?

If you'd like a simple tool to help you create the budget, download our budget template in Excel by visiting: https://financiallysimple.com/personal-budget

#6 - CREATE A TRANSITION BUDGET

As you are creating a retirement budget, you also need to prepare a transition budget. Throughout the years, you have been investing money into your business. Yet, you cannot just cash-out that investment and run. Selling your business is a process, and you will have to invest money in the right professionals and into "renovations" in order to sell it. Decide now how much money you can spend and how much money you are willing to invest in the sales process to convert your ill-liquid asset into a liquid asset.

#7 - FINE-TUNE YOUR ESTATE PLAN

Now is also a great time to take another look at your will in case you need to make changes to it. If you don't have a will, talk to your attorney immediately and make one. No one is guaranteed tomorrow, so you are taking a major, unnecessary risk if you do not have a will in place to determine what happens to your life's savings, your home, and your assets upon your death.

If you will be leaving considerable wealth to family members or friends, they could owe estate taxes on your "gifts." Therefore, you want to talk to your attorney, your CPA, and your CFP® to minimize your loved ones' tax liabilities and burdens.

#8 - DECIDE HOW MUCH LONGER YOU NEED TO WORK

Unless you've experienced a financial windfall that has fortified your financial livelihood for the rest of your life, you will probably have to stretch limited money over your retirement years and give up some of your retirement goals, or you will have to work longer to save and pay for those dreams. As you are writing down your retirement goals, determining when to draw your Social Security benefits, reallocating your investments, fine tuning your estate plans, and preparing your retirement budget, consider how many more years of work are necessary for you to reach your objectives.

LET YOUR ADVISORY TEAM GUIDE YOUR RETIREMENT PLANS

Preparing for retirement is hard. You do not know how many years you'll have left on earth once you retire, nor do you know how healthy you'll be to experience retirement. Thus, much of your data is based on subjective numbers. For that reason, if for no others, you'll want to rely on your professional advisory team to guide you through your retirement preparations. They can help you budget, save, plan, and fine tune. They can look at your current numbers and help you decide how much longer you need to work.

Then, once you know how much longer you need to work, you can determine how many more months or years you need to invest time and energy into your business. Can you prepare yourself and your business for the Ultimate Sale within 10 years? Can you retire earlier than that, or will you be working 20 to 30 more years? Whatever your retirement timeline is, you need to invest in your personal assets and in your business's assets.

I have briefly discussed saving your personal money in retirement accounts and in other savings accounts. I've talked about paying down debt, cutting expenses, waiting for Social Security benefits and more to help you personally prepare for retirement. While you are implementing your retirement savings' plans, it is time to begin evaluating and building the value of your business.

CHAPTER 4

TEST THE SOUNDNESS OF YOUR STRUCTURE

"Do not worry if you have built your castles in the air. They are where they should be. Now put the foundations under them."

Henry David Thoreau

PLANNING YOUR EXIT

Many business owners believe that business **exit planning**, or *the idea of preparing a business to sell*, occurs around the time the final sale takes place. Perhaps, proprietors think they can begin preparing their company for sale one or two months beforehand. Based on my experience, this could not be further from the truth, especially if there is a gap in the market value and the desired value the business owner is seeking.

As a business owner, you need to begin planning your exit from your business years before you plan to retire and/or list your business for sale. Most notably, once you develop a vision of what your business's sale and proceeds will look like, you've assembled your advisory team, and you've assessed your personal savings and retirement goals, you need to review your company's structural logistics, starting with its entity status.

A few years ago, one of my clients, who I will call "Sally," ran into an unusual business dilemma directly relating to the type of business entity she chose prior to ever working with me. Sally was a successful businesswoman who worked hard and built an amazing company. One day, completely out of the blue, a buyer stopped in and made Sally an unbelievable offer to buy her business. This was a once-in-a-lifetime dream offer. After receiving an official, written offer, Sally contacted my office for exit planning guidance.

Scrambling, I assembled an exit team. Through my company, Heritage Investors, I stepped into the role of the Certified Exit Planning Advisor, and a team member within my company served as the CERTIFIED FINANCIAL PLANNER™. I also added a qualified business attorney and a Certified Public Accountant to the exit planning team. As we began reviewing the buyer's offer and the business owner's financial statements, the team and I quickly recognized a problem that revolved around the *type* of business entity Sally had formed. As her business was currently structured, Sally's business would pay taxes upon the sale. Then, Sally would pay taxes on the remainder of the proceeds on a personal level. Called double taxation, it seemed like highway robbery to Sally.

Obviously, Sally did not sell her business at that time. Instead, we put together a long-term business exit plan to help her sell her business in 10 years' time with fewer tax ramifications.

FOUR BASIC TYPES OF BUSINESS ENTITIES

Like Sally's, your chosen business structure will prove important to buyers looking to purchase your company now or 10 years from now. For example, let us say that you operate your company as a C Corporation that files and pays its own taxes separately from your personal taxes. A potential buyer who wants to buy a business that allows pass-through taxation may choose to walk away from buying any business like yours. Such a buyer might even purchase a competitor's company. Therefore, operating as the "right" type of entity matters a great deal for your future sellability.

While I will provide you with a list of the types of business entities under which you can operate, you will want to consult your own professional team of attorneys, CFPs®, and CPAs to know which entity will provide you the best leverage to sell your company. Before you decide to keep or change your entity status, you will want to understand what each entity offers your business. Here are the four basic types of business entities:

- C Corporations
- S Corporations, a.k.a. Sub-Chapter S Corporations

- Partnerships
- Limited Liability Companies, a.k.a. LLCs

A fifth type of business exists, but since it is not a state-recognized business entity, I did not include it in my list. If you do not form your company as one of the above entities, then you are operating a sole proprietorship. Although it is a business, it is not a *type* of business entity. As you look at selling a business, you want to be aware of that disadvantage.

USING YOUR BUSINESS STRUCTURE TO LEVERAGE YOUR SELLABILITY

Each type of business entity has advantages and disadvantages. Remember my client, Sally? Had she filed one document, she could have moved her company from a double taxation system into a single taxation system pretty easily. With just one form, folks. Therefore, the type of entity under which you operate your business matters. Ultimately, you will choose to operate as an entity, and your future business's buyer will show interest in your company for one, or several, of the following reasons:

Personal Liability Protection

Operating your business under a corporate veil will protect your personal assets should your business run into problems. Additionally, running a company as a recognized business entity can reduce personal exposure to risk and act as a hedge of protection over and above what business insurance can provide.

Transference of Stock or Membership Interest

Within C Corps or S Corps, you can divide stock, move stock, or transfer stock among owners or investors with some limitations. You can even give certain types of stock to employees. In an LLC, members (the owners) can rearrange, divide, reallocate, or transfer membership interests.

Flexibility

Vital to entrepreneurs, business entities allow owners to manage their companies as they see fit. They provide flexibility over the ownership structure that allows the company to move and flow as individual owner's circumstances do.

Tax Reduction Strategies

With the help of a tax planning professional like a CPA, business owners can take advantage of tax-free fringe benefits available to business entities. They can also prevent double taxation issues or plan how much they'll pay in taxes by operating as an entity and by getting help from an accountant. Yes, tax planning happens. As a business owner, you can regulate the amount of taxes you pay, but tax planning requires effort and continuous help from your advisory team.

ADD STRUCTURAL REINFORCEMENTS

When you and your Dream Team of advisors review your original business entity selection, you will analyze it for structural and operational soundness in relation to its future sellability. Does your chosen entity provide a future buyer with enough protection, flexibility, membership interest, and tax reduction strategies? If it does not, you need to research which type of entity will. Then, with the help of your professional advisors, you will work with your state agency to change your entity status.

However, if you determine that you are operating under the "right" type of business entity for sellability, you are not off the hook yet. Not at all. You need to make sure you have your structural reinforcements in place. Are your original operational ownership agreements signed and in force? Do you have those documents handy, and have you reviewed them for accuracy? As you look over these business documents, your advising attorney will be a vital source of information and help. He will ensure that the following agreements are written in such a way that future buyers can seamlessly purchase your business without hiccups over ownership percentages, partner disputes, or restrictive transference agreements.

An Operating Agreement

Also known as a Partnership Agreement, the Operating Agreement is a document that addresses how your company will handle owner disagreements. It specifies who will fill which role and how the company will be managed. Additionally, it outlines how and where the company will file lawsuits, and it deals with tax allocation, income disbursements, and disposition (sale or closure) of the company. Written with vast detail or in relatively simple terms, the agreement protects business owners should crisis ensue and ensures potential buyers that owners have done due diligence to protect themselves and the business.

Buy-Sell Agreement

Additionally, many lawyers and planners will recommend that their business owner clients draw up a Buy-Sell Agreement. Whether you have multiple owners, or majority and minority shareholders, you must agree to sell the company and to work toward that end. With this type of document, you can dictate how the company will be sold, the method of valuation to be used to determine minimum sales price, and under what arrangement it will be sold. This agreement also addresses what happens to the company in the event of an owner's death or disability. Although not required by law, if you are building a company to sell, the very title of the Buy-Sell Agreement seems to recommend its use.

KEEP DETAILED RECORDS

Even though you and your team of professionals have approved or drawn up the foundational business documents your company may need, you still have work to do on your entity selection. At this point in time, you must maintain your business entity. You need to document, document, document. Accurately recording business transactions and keeping up with those records can spare you heartache and loss if you end up running into legal battles in the future, and it can make future buyers more confident in your company's operations.

Then, what other types of owner activities warrant documentation?

- Issuing stock shares
- Selling stock shares
- Loaning the company money
- Borrowing money from the company
- Placing the company in debt
- Meeting minutes

From legal issues to meeting minutes, you might want to document anything that happens as it relates to the company's operation. Consult your advisory team to determine what types of records your business needs to keep regarding its entity status.

CHAPTER 5

DUST OFF YOUR BUSINESS'S BLUEPRINTS

"Nobody ever wrote down a plan to be broke, fat, lazy, or stupid. Those things are what happen when you don't have a plan."

Larry Winget

BLUEPRINTS COMMUNICATE VISION

While you and your Dream Team of advisors are reviewing your business's chosen entity type, you also need to look at your business's "blueprints." Blueprints are most often seen at construction sites and are detailed drawings of buildings on huge pieces of paper. More specifically, Wikipedia calls a blueprint a "reproduction of a technical drawing, documenting an architecture or an engineering design."[12] Those drawings "document," or *plan out*, every part of the building's structure, showing dimensions and placements of rooms, doors, windows, studs, cabinets, plumbing, outlets, stairways, walls, and every other aspect of the building. Essentially, architects, builders, or engineers use blueprints as their "method of communication" to show contracted workers exactly where to place the structural elements for aesthetic and structural soundness.[13]

What if you hired an architect to design your dream house but he never showed you what the house would look like? Without a blueprint to review, how would you know for sure you liked it? The architect's vision of a colonial style house could be completely different than your idea of what a colonial

12 Wikipedia. (n.d.) Blueprint. Retrieved from https://en.wikipedia.org/wiki/Blueprint
13 What Exactly is a Blueprint? (n.d.). Retrieved from https://science.howstuffworks.com/engineering/structural/question321.htm

house should look like, but you would never know unless you saw his drawings of the house.

Additionally, without a blueprint, builders would have no way to determine whether all the puzzle pieces of rooms, doors, windows, cabinets, and decks fit together properly. For that matter, the contractors and subcontractors would have no instructions for how to fit the puzzle pieces of the house together either. You cannot verbally explain how you want a house to look and expect multiple contractors and subcontractors to interpret your vision in the same manner.

YOUR BUSINESS PLAN IS YOUR BUSINESS'S BLUEPRINT

Like builders, business owners need blueprints to *plan* their business's success. Essentially, writing down a business plan allows others to see the vision in your mind clearly, and it provides a matrix to determine whether your business has become successful. At its simplest, the business plan is an official statement of your company's objectives, the reasoning behind your objectives, and the strategies you will use to successfully fulfill your objectives. It puts the vision in your mind into a form that others can understand.

When you reach the point where you want to act on selling your business, those around you who will help you through this process will need to understand your specific vision. How will you, your spouse, your employees, and your advisory team know which direction to go if you haven't clearly defined the specific vision you desire as the owner of the company? How will buyers know what your intentions were and are for your business? What is its purpose? How does it operate? What does it sell? What systems does it use? How do each of the pieces fit together? What will success look like? Basically, you want everyone from the buyer to your employees to grasp the vision of the business.

You also want to have a written business plan, or blueprint, so that your advisory team and potential buyers can review every aspect of your business at one time to evaluate its current worth. You will need to draw parallels between the various areas of your business to see if you've missed a piece of the puzzle. Let's say that your business has one salesperson but as you write out your business plan, you realize you need to sell 20,000 widgets by year end to have a sellable business. You know what? Your one salesperson is probably not going to be able to sell 20,000 widgets in 12 months alone. By comparing sales and marketing goals to your company's people and operations, you can catch that problem and fix it before you put your business on the market.

Finally, you want to write out a business plan so that you can forecast the future of your company. By analyzing your business's historical growth, expansion, employee turnover, product turnover, company systems, and more, you can correctly forecast your company's future. Examining where your company has been, where it is now, and where it has the potential to go entices buyers looking to invest money into buying your business. How can a buyer determine a return on investment or the expected timeframe of the return if he has no documentable growth and expansion rates to examine? If you cannot provide buyers with visual representations and proof worthy of an investment of capital, potential buyers will never get past your business plan and make an offer to purchase.

TAKE THE TIME TO WRITE THE PLAN

I advise business owners to begin their businesses by writing out a business plan. However, if you are considering selling your company and do not have a formal business plan written, take the time to do it now. You might believe that writing down your objectives will be a waste of time. After all, if *you* know every element of your business and can tell anyone who asks, why do you need to write it down, especially if you are already 10, 20, or 30 years into business? Candidly, *you* are the problem. As you will see in Chapter 26, you must move the company away from *you* being the be-all and end-all. To communicate your vision successfully to others, you need to write down a plan for your business just like your architect needs to draw up blueprints for buildings.

I challenge you to stop right now. No matter how beautiful you think your business is, it will not interest any buyer if it does not follow a plan for success or identify what success looks like. Make time to write out a business plan. Do not work towards your business's sale without direction. Instead, work on your business's direction to help it sell.

CHAPTER 6

UPDATE YOUR BLUEPRINTS[14]

"If the plan doesn't work, change the plan, not the goal."

Unknown

Now that you know why you need a formalized business plan, you need to know what to look for as you and your team are evaluating your business for structural soundness. In general, business professionals suggest that entrepreneurs include five, seven, or nine categories within their written business plans. I particularly like the structure of a nine-part business plan, but the number of categories you include or the arrangement of those categories does not matter as much as the functionality of your plan. Is it a working, living document that potential buyers can refer to again and again for direction and motivation? If not, tweak it; rewrite it. Look at the plan from a buyer's perspective and revise it accordingly.

I'll list the nine categories I see used most often in business plans, but ultimately, you and your advisors must decide what works best for your business as you prepare for its sale.

#1 - COMPANY DESCRIPTION

In this section, you will want to explain who you are, how you operate, and what your goals are. Write down basic information like the name and location of your business. Include the type of structure or business entity you have

---

14 For more information on a business plan, visit https://financiallysimple.com/financially-simple-guide-good-business-plan/

chosen and a brief history of the business. Who started the company? Why did you start the company? When did it open for business? What products or services do you offer? How does your company meet a supply or demand?

In the company description, I have even seen some companies talk about specific, best-selling products or significant, big-name customers. Basically, friends, this part just summarizes everything about your company—the who, the what, the where, the when, and the how.

#2 - PRODUCTS AND SERVICES

You have already identified your product or service offerings in the company description, but in this section, you should provide more detailed information about your product or service. What are you selling? How does your product meet customer needs? What benefit does your service provide to the marketplace? How long does your product last? What does your service cost? Did you do any research and development (R&D) to get the product off the ground? If so, what did you do? In this category, you may even want to include details about your vendors and suppliers because if you can identify your product costs and product sale prices, you can theoretically predict revenue from product sales.

You also want to discuss your company's intellectual property here. For instance, do you hold patents, trademarks, or copyrights on any of your products or services? Have you created a process that will make your product costs lower than your competitors' costs? Do you have a unique food or chemical recipe that sets your product apart in the industry? If you hold intellectual property, mention each, but save the document files, patent pictures, special ingredients, or process diagrams for the Appendix section we will discuss shortly.

#3 - MARKET ANALYSIS

Next is perhaps the most difficult and lengthy section of a business plan. You can describe your products and services all day long. Yet, when it comes to completing a statistical overview of your industry norms and the customers you target, you get hung up. By pressing on through this section, though, potential buyers will gain a better understanding of who your target market is and how your business makes an impact within your industry's current marketplace.

Start with a historical overview of your industry. Pay particular attention to the expansion and development of your products or services. Then, once you've given an account of your marketplace, identify your target within it. What type of customer needs your products? Can anyone use your products, or do they only apply to a specific consumer niche? What characteristics do your customers have in common, and why do they need your services?

When you have identified your customer type within your marketplace, you can focus on how you broke into that marketplace. What do your direct and indirect competitors do well or poorly? Do you outsource your product manufacturing to lower your costs and increase your profit margins? Do your products or services fill a void within a specific industry?

Last within your market analysis, you want to list any regulations you must follow that affect your products or services. Do you have to meet specific HIPAA or OSHA standards? Have you taken a Hippocratic Oath, or do you have fiduciary responsibilities to your clients? Do you have to maintain food-grade kitchen standards? Listing and understanding the standards you must uphold within your company will help interested buyers know which local, regional, and national laws they will have to navigate if they purchase your company.

#4 - MARKETING AND SALES

In this section, you want to explain how you have positioned your product or service to your prospective customers. It is that simple. What type of media have you used to promote your products and services, and what are you using now? Do you use word-of-mouth advertising, or do you use printed advertisements or social media to reach new customers? Have you filmed TV commercials or recorded radio advertisements? Have direct mailers gotten your name into more homes than coupons in your local newspaper?

How often do you advertise? Do you have an advertising budget? What are your average expenditures for marketing? Do you have current monthly, quarterly, or yearly contracts with advertising agents? Can you identify how much income your advertising dollars bring into the company?

Assuming your advertising has been effective, how did you scale your business internally and externally to accommodate the increasing sales, product demand, customer base, client base, or patient base? Do you have systems in place to expand or to contract quickly if demand for your product or service changes?

Speaking of sales, do you have a way to capture customer data for additional marketing efforts of new products or services your company offers or develops? Then once you develop that new product or service, what types of quality assurance practices have you put in place, and what are the results of those practices? Do you offer additional quality assurance through warranties on your products or services? Can you then track the percentage of product returns and give details about them? Finally, how does your service department track its effectiveness and success?

Ultimately, your marketing and sales departments should work together. One promotes the quality of your products and services while the other ensures the quality of the products and services you sell. If you can promote AND ensure quality, then sales of your products and services should increase.

#5 - ORGANIZATIONAL STRUCTURE, OWNERSHIP, AND MANAGEMENT

Next within your business plan, you want to tell who is involved in your business, what role each plays in the company, and the credentials each brings to the table. Start with company ownership. How many people own the company? Who are the owners? What is their background and history? How are ownership percentages divided? Do owners hold equity equivalents like stocks, securities, or warrants that can be redeemed, traded, or sold?

Does the type of business entity you have chosen require you to have a board of directors or corporate officers? Who are they? What is their background and area of expertise? How often do they meet, and what qualifies them to offer owners advice? Do they play a role in the managerial operations of your company?

Who runs your company? What is their pedigree, and what do you pay them? Do you offer benefit, bonus, or retirement plans to your managers or employees? How do you handle hiring and firing?

Do you have other professionals as part of your planning team? Who are they, and what are their credentials? Does a certain CPA give you tax advice, and does a CERTIFIED FINANCIAL PLANNER™ provide your company with long-term strategic planning guidance? Do you have a go-to business lawyer on your team?

If you have a complex infrastructure, you may want to provide a flow chart that shows your ownership, organizational, and managerial hierarchies. In it, you can provide details about who oversees decisions and what type of decisions they make.

#6 - FUNDING

Vital to potential investors in your company or purchasers of your company, this Request-for-Funding section must outline how much capital you needed to begin your business and how you funded strategic initiatives over the life of the business. Go into detail about how you used funding and the results of the deployed capital. If you have not borrowed money, you want to explain how you arrived where you are and where you spent the money within your company.

If you borrowed money, how have you repaid it? Have you tarnished your company's name or credit history by making late payments or by refusing to pay at all? Did you make repayments from your cash flow, or did you have to take out a loan to pay down other debts? Does your business make enough money to pay back loans?

Have you acquired other businesses, assets, or products? Do you plan to sell the business as a possible means to pay down outstanding debt?

#7 - FINANCIAL PROJECTIONS

Since you are hoping to convince potential buyers to purchase your company, you want to record all past and current financial details and then tabulate your business's assumptive growth rate in a pro forma.[15] Use your known financials *conservatively* to estimate future financial growth. If you inflate your projections, you could lose the trust of lenders or buyers, losing potential capital or profits. Therefore, outline your current and past financials as accurately as possible so that you can provide realistic estimates of future financials.

How exactly do you do that? Well, in something like an Excel spreadsheet, list all recurring monthly, quarterly, and yearly expenses your company incurs and the income you expect to receive on a daily, weekly, monthly, quarterly, and yearly basis. Do you operate from an established budget? Do you have plans and resources to cover unexpected expenditures? Then, using the growth rate your spreadsheet already shows, predict the financial growth of your company over the next year, two years, three years, or more.

#8 - APPENDIX

While this section does not plan or predict growth, it provides documentation and evidence you need to show interested buyers. This appendix is not like a book appendix that everyone needs to see for references. No, this section is often restricted to a need-to-know basis for investors, creditors, partners, and buyers. Because it includes proprietary and confidential information, only your closest advisors, investors, or potential buyers who have signed the proper non-disclosure documents need to see this part of your business plan.

You may have your credit history and your market analysis within the appendix. Do you really want those things in the hands of your competitors? Not at all! You may have letters of references, patents, permits, trademarks, copyrights, and leases in the section. Staff resumes and contracts could be within this section, too.

---

15 For a sample pro forma, visit https://financiallysimple.com/pro-forma-financial-statements/

Although this information will be vital to potential buyers, you do not need to show it to your employees or anyone else outside of your advisory team.

#9 - EXECUTIVE SUMMARY

Arguably the most critical section of your business plan is its one- to two-page executive summary. Even though it will appear at the beginning of your business plan, you should write it after the other sections to bring everything together. At its most basic, the executive summary will tell the readers the history of your company, where it is today, the direction it is headed, and where you see potential for success. You want to catch potential buyers' attention from the beginning of the plan so that they will continue reading it and remain interested in your company.

TURN A GOOD BUSINESS PLAN INTO A *GREAT* BUSINESS PLAN

As you write down your business plans or as you review them with your advisory team from a buyer's perspective, remember to use them as your business's blueprint. Clarity is key. *Clearly* outline who is involved and what role each plays so that management lines do not blur. Refer to your market niche to show that you are master of one thing rather than mediocre at all things. Use the business plan to set yourself apart from your competition and to quantify your own business's success. Then, show potential buyers how you accomplished your plan or how they can bring your plans to fruition. Ultimately, this blueprint of your company's plans and successes could be the difference between your success or failure to sell your business.

EVALUATE YOUR CURRENT WORTH

"Price is what you pay. Value is what you get."
Warren Buffet

O nce you decide to sell your business, you must know what makes it valuable to buyers because not all worth is quantifiable.

CHAPTER 7

UNDERSTAND WHAT MAKES YOUR BUSINESS VALUABLE

*"Too many people undervalue what they are
and overvalue what they're not."*

KUSHANDWIZDOM

WHAT IS YOUR BUSINESS WORTH?

One of the very first questions I field whenever I start working with new clients is "Justin, how much do you think my business is worth?" Perhaps, as you are assessing your business's structural elements, you are asking your advisory team the same question. I hear people ask it all the time, and it is a valid question, especially if you want to sell your business.

You know, **the truth of the matter is that your business is worth whatever someone is willing to pay for it**. End of story. That's all folks.

At this point, I can hear my dad's voice telling me, "Now son, that's a cop-out answer." You may want to tell me the same thing. However, no matter which type of approach you use for your calculations or how many different calculations you run, the only thing that matters is how much someone gives you for the business. Let me take you through an example in my life.

STICKER SHOCK

In 2012, my wife and I decided to sell our house. Having grown tired of suburbia, we wanted to move to the country, live on a farm, drive tractors, play with goats and chickens, and raise our children. As we prepared to list the house, we scheduled a meeting with a REALTOR®. When this professional friend of mine got to the house, she already had the listing paperwork drawn up. She sat down with us and addressed that most important question first. She said, "Well guys, how much are we going to sell the house for?"

Now I was ready for that question. I *knew* how much my house was worth, so I gave her a number. Without hesitation, the REALTOR® looked at me and said, "Um, yeah. I don't think so, Justin," and she quoted me the price she believed my house was worth. Hearing her valuation was like hearing a gunshot going off in my ear, and all I heard was ringing. After I picked myself up off the floor, I said, "Do you realize that number is $20,000 less than I paid for the house *before* I finished the basement and did many other home improvements?!?"

To this day, I still remember what she said next: "While that may be true, you will never sell it for more than this price in this current housing market." You know what? She was right. We stayed in that house for about three more years to allow the housing market to recover just to break even on the house.

WHAT MAKES MY BUSINESS VALUABLE?

Like many business owners, I thought my house was more valuable than it was. I ignorantly assumed it was worth *at least* the money I had invested in it.

At this point in time, you have decided to sell your business, and you have assembled your advisory team. Before the team ever met, you probably had an ideal sales price in mind for your business like I did for my house. If you are like other business professionals I have met, you want to *make* money when you sell your company; you don't want to lose it. That would make no sense. No one wants to lose money. You as an entrepreneur, especially, want to make a return on your investment, and you do not want to settle for anything less than the best rate of return.

As you have "patiently" watched your team members analyze your business entity and your business plan for structural soundness, you have been waiting for them to evaluate the worth of your business. You cannot wait to hear how much money you will make when you sell. But what parts of your business are valuable? What makes your business attractive to buyers?

Well, your *capital* makes your business attractive to buyers, but capital is not just "cash." Capital is defined as "wealth in the form of money or assets, taken as a sign of the financial strength of an...organization...and assumed to be available for development or investment."[16]

In other words, *capital is the various forms of "wealth" or assets within your company*. Thus, the question "What parts of your business are valuable?" becomes interchangeable with the question "What types of capital exist within your business?"

THE THREE FORMS OF CAPITAL

As I see it, there are three basic forms of capital, or wealth, within your business that help determine its value—your cash flow, your tangible assets, and your intangible assets. The value of your business and the value of your assets are inextricably linked together, so we must understand what your capital assets are to calculate your business's value.

Cash Flow

You have heard the expression "cash is king." Well, in this instance, that is true. Before buyers look at anything else in your business, they want to see the amount of money your business makes. They want to know how much money comes into a business compared to how much money goes out of it. They are looking at your cash flow. What are your yearly gross sales? How much revenue is left after you subtract your business's expenses from its gross sales? Sure, your business may "make" tons of money, but did you spend more than you made? Were your expenses necessary or frivolous? Are you able to pay yourself, or are you still putting money in each month to make ends meet?

16 Business Dictionary. Capital. (n.d.) Retrieved from http://www.businessdictionary.com/ definition/capital.html

Tangible Assets

Buyers will also look at your material assets to help determine how valuable your company is to them. When I think of tangible assets, I think of the items your business owns that you can physically remove from your building or which you can put a price tag on.[17] These things include cash on hand, accounts receivable, furniture, fixtures, equipment, inventory, automobiles, technological devices, and real estate owned. Your tangible assets can be quantified and compared to other businesses within your industry, and they can be sold for cash within your marketplace.

Intangible Assets

More difficult to price, yet arguably more valuable to a buyer than your tangible assets, are your intangible assets. A business's intangible assets come in the form of employees, customers, performance, systems, culture, brand recognition, intellectual property, independence from the owner, transferability, and reputation.[18]

Unlike your cash flow or your tangible assets, your intangible assets are not easy to quantify. For example, no single software system or financial statement can calculate precisely how valuable your brand recognition is in your marketplace or how valuable it will be to business buyers. However, as I mentioned above, the intangibles often make your business more valuable than tangible assets.

RISK FACTORS AFFECT YOUR CAPITAL

Although you want to show a potential business buyer all the assets and value within your company, a buyer will also be looking at your liabilities, or the amount of risk your company has assumed. Many of those liabilities will show

17 White, Jeff. How to Value a Business: The Ultimate Guide to Business Valuation. (January 2018). Retrieved from https://fitsmallbusiness.com/how-to-value-a-business/
18 White, Jeff. How to Value a Business: The Ultimate Guide to Business Valuation. (January 2018). Retrieved from https://fitsmallbusiness.com/how-to-value-a-business/

up on your financial statements (i.e. equipment loans, building leases, credit card debt, accounts payable, payroll taxes owed, sales taxes owed, etc.), but some of your business's liabilities come in intangible form.

Factors outside of your control like the natural environment, your geographic and regional locale, the current political climate, and economic booms or crashes can also determine how much risk your business poses for potential buyers. Since you cannot control those risk factors, though, your job as business owner trying to sell your company is to keep your known and controllable liabilities low. What buyer wants to assume excessive credit card debt or loans on equipment that is 10 years old?

CHAPTER 8

APPRAISE YOUR BUSINESS'S CURRENT WORTH

"Don't be afraid to convince yourself that your business is incredible,
but don't expect others to be convinced without solid data to back it up."

Palmer Luckey

Now that you have identified the three basic forms of capital that exist within your business and understand that risk factors can raise or lower the value of your capital, you and your advisory team can assign a type or several types of value to the business you will be selling.

Let's start by identifying the various types of "value" that can be assigned to your business and/or its assets.

- **Replacement Value** – Based on the age and condition of your tangible assets, replacement value is how much it would cost a buyer to replace your furniture and fixtures, your materials and supplies, your equipment, your merchandise, your computers and technology, or your building, if they were destroyed or stolen.

- **Book Value** – Taken from your business's balance sheet, book value is essentially the amount of money you paid for your tangible assets minus their depreciated value or plus their appreciated value.

- **Liquidation Value** – If a judge forces you to dissolve your company, its assets, and its stock holdings to pay creditors or claimants against you, liquidation value is the amount of money your tangible assets would garner in a short sale.

- **Collateral Value** – If a business buyer takes out a loan to purchase your business, the lending institution will often use the company's assets as collateral should the buyer default on the loan. If the business loses value after the purchase, the lender may require the buyer to provide additional assets to "underpin" the loan, which could be problematic.[19]

- **Fair Market Value** – In *Financially Simple* terms, fair market value refers to the price a willing buyer, who is wholly unaffiliated with your company, would pay for your business.[20] In this valuation, buyers compare your company with other companies in your industry to determine what your company is worth to them. Often called an arm's length value, fair market value "is commonly used to value businesses or business interests for sale and tax purposes" in a hypothetical environment.[21]

- **Market Value** – Similar to and sometimes interchangeable with fair market value, market value also refers to sales between business owners and people unaffiliated with the business owner or with the business. However, it focuses on probable or realized value rather than potential value.[22] For instance, appraisers using this valuation will determine your company's value by comparing it to the price for which other companies sold within your marketplace and geographic location.

- **Fair Value** – Most often used in financial reporting or litigation, companies must undergo an IRS Section 409A valuation by an appraiser to determine their stocks' off-market value if they plan to offer stock options to employees or contractors, or if they must sell

19 Wall Street Oasis. What is Collateral Value? (n.d.). Retrieved from https://www.wallstreetoasis.com/finance-dictionary/what-is-collateral-value
20 IRS Revenue Ruling 59-60. (1959). Retrieved from http://www.equityvaluationappraisals.com/pdf/IRS-Revenue-Ruling-59-60.pdf
21 MBAP Certified Public Accountants and Advisors. Know the Difference Between Fair Market Value and Fair Value. (2017). Retrieved from https://mbafcpa.com/advisories/know-differences-fair-market-value-fair-value/
22 Maloney, Dave. Market Value vs. Fair Market Value: What's the Difference. (October 2012). Retrieved from https://www.appraisalcourseassociates.com/1265/

or transfer privately held stocks to settle a business partnership or personal spousal dispute.[23]

- **Investment Value** – Possibly higher or lower than fair market value, investment value is the amount of money an investor is willing to pay for a business according to the investor's own judgements and assumptions.[24] Typically, the investor bases valuation on the return on investment, or ROI, the investor expects to receive from the company.

- **Strategic Value** – Synergistic in nature, strategic value is the amount a competitor, an investor, or another company will pay for your assets to "get rid of" their competition or to combine assets to form a powerhouse company able to dominate a niche marketplace.[25] Often, this type of valuation leads to the highest price a seller will get because a buyer needs something (to eliminate competition or to join forces with the competition) and is willing to pay to get it.

Your business or assets can be quantified and compared to other businesses within your industry, and they can be sold for cash within your marketplace. Business appraisers can place a numerical value on your business or assets using one *or many* appraisal methods.

THE THREE MOST COMMON FORMS OF BUSINESS VALUATION

The Asset Approach

If your tangible assets are more valuable than your intangible assets or more impressive than your business's cash flow, you may choose to list those physical items for sale rather than your business.

---

23 Kim, Larry. 7 Things You Need to Know about 409A Valuation. (December 2017). Retrieved from https://medium.com/marketing-and-entrepreneurship/7-things-you-need-to-know-about-409a-valuation-35d4da0fa58a

24 Valuation Academy. Types of Value - Fair Market Value, Intrinsic Value, Liquidation Value, Investment Value. (n.d.). Retrieved from http://valuationacademy.com/types-of-value/

25 Mendlowitz, Edward. Uncover Strategic Value. (2009). Retrieved from https://www.journalofaccountancy.com/issues/2009/nov/20092092.html

For example, I have a client who owns an outdoor excavating business, and if he ever sells it, he will basically be selling the bulldozers, backhoes, loaders, skid steers, graders, trenchers, and other equipment he uses to do business and nothing more. Another client of mine owns a medical office building, and he wants to sell the building but keep running his dental practice within that building. Therefore, he would sell his real estate asset but not his business.

In an asset sale, appraisers will usually place a price on the business's tangible property based on one of the following *types of value: its replacement value, its book value, its liquidation value or its collateral value.*

Although an asset sale can be fairly easy to calculate, it also tends to bring the lowest sales price because appraisers are only looking at one form of your business's capital—your tangible assets, which includes the company's good-will. Here's what that equation looks like:

Business Assets + Goodwill = Business Value

If you believe your intangible assets and your cash flow bring added value to your business, you may want to appraise your businesses using a market approach or an income approach.

The Market Approach

When our REALTOR® dropped the bomb on my dreams to sell my house back in 2012, she was prepared to offer evidence for why she valued the house $20,000 below what I paid for it. When I managed to stutter, "How'd you figure that price?" my real estate agent promptly replied, "Here. Here's a list of what the houses that are similar to yours have sold for in your area." She had prepared a list of comparable houses, or "comps," that recently sold near ours with the same number of bedrooms, the same number of bathrooms, and a similar square footage. Because she knew what people were paying for those houses, she could determine what buyers would expect to pay for mine.

Similarly, professionals can compare sales prices or estimated values of similar businesses or similar businesses' tangible assets within your marketplace to determine your business's listing price based on one of the following *types of value: its Fair Market Value, its Market Value, its fair value, its investment value, or its strategic value.*

In a market approach, an appraiser will often calculate your business's sales price based on the average value of three comparable businesses within your industry within your vicinity. For instance, if Company A two blocks away sold for $1 million, Company B on your street sold for $2 million, and Company C a mile away sold for $1.25 million, then an appraiser might recommend that you list your company for roughly $1.42 million, the average value of the three companies. Thus, the market approach calculation looks like this:

Average of Market Comps = Business Value

However, there is an inherent weakness within this type of valuation – the right to privacy. You see, small businesses do not have transparency requirements, and owners tend to keep their business operations and dealings to themselves. Unless you have the "inside scoop" on your competitor's business, you cannot realistically compare your company's worth to the other company's sales price.

Just because a company three miles down the street from yours sold for $2 million doesn't mean your company is worth the same $2 million. Your company may have better equipment, stronger intangible assets, and a deeper customer base. Wouldn't that mean your company was worth more than $2 million? Again, there is no way to adequately compare the two companies unless you and your appraiser have inside information about both companies.

Unfortunately, though, business brokers and business owners often use the market approach when they are evaluating a business's worth because it is a relatively "easy" one to calculate.

The Income Approach

As we arrive at this third approach, we reach the appraisal method most professional business appraisers use to calculate a business's value on behalf of buyers and sellers alike. Essentially, when appraisers use an income approach, they look at a **business's past, present, and future** *cash earnings (its income)* to determine its base value. Although that may sound simple, determining a business's worth through an income approach is an incredibly complex process that involves proper selection, calculation, and use of the capitalization rate, the discount rate, and valuation multiples.

To begin, the appraiser will formulate a business's value through its capitalization rate, or its "Cap Rate." Essentially, this calculation predicts the return on investment (ROI) a buyer is likely to receive from the purchase of the business based on its **historic returns**. For instance, let's say that a landscaping business generates $300,000 in net operating income (NOI) each year, and the business has a list price of $1.5 million. The Cap Rate is calculated by dividing $300,000 (the NOI) by $1.5 million (the list price) which equals 0.2 or 20 percent. Thus, if a buyer purchases the company, he would likely receive a 20 percent rate of return (assuming he did not use a loan to purchase the business).

Essentially, then, the capitalization rate calculation looks like this:

**Annual Future Earnings ÷ Required Rate of Return
= Business Value**

Next, an appraiser will use the income-based discounted cash flow valuation method to formulate business value as a **future** income stream discounted to the present value. In this method, the appraiser will analyze the company's discount rate, or the rate of return required to make the business a worthy investment for the buyer. In other words, you compare the rate of return an investor *could* make in the future by purchasing the business to the returns the buyer *could* make by investing the money into other assets.

For instance, let's assume that a Certificate of Deposit yields a 3 percent return, a government bond yields a 5 percent return, a diversified equity portfolio yields an 8 percent return, a loan to your sweet nephew yields a 10 percent return, and the purchase of the landscaping company yields a 20 percent return on your investment. Each of these investments has its own specific risk, but the discount rate helps the buyer determine if the purchase of the business with its assumed rate of return is worth the risk incurred.

Thus, the discounted rate calculation looks like something like this:

Cash Flow During First Year
÷ (Required Rate of Return – Growth Rate)
= Business Value

The final determination method appraisers use as part of the Income valuation approach is the Multiple of Discretionary Earnings Method. Although the capitalization rate looks at past performance and brings it to the present and the discount rate looks at potential future performance and brings it to the present, the valuation Multiple Method looks at the present.

To determine a company's value through multiple valuation, an appraiser takes business earnings and multiples them by a multiple. Sounds simple, right? Yet, what complicates this method is that the appraiser could use gross revenue, gross profit, net income, net profit, cash flow, book value, Earnings Before Income Taxes Depreciation and Amortization (EBITDA), Earnings Before Income and Taxes (EBIT), Seller's Discretionary Earnings (SDE), business assets, or owner's equity to represent the company's earnings. Then, the appraiser arrives at a multiplier based on specific business factors, industry factors, market factors, and owner's insights OR by dividing the sales price by the company's earnings.

Eventually, the Multiple of Discretionary Earnings Method calculation will look something like this:

Company Earnings x Multiplier = Business Value

Although *business appraisers use a combination of capitalization rates, discount rates, AND valuation multiple methods to arrive at the most accurate, present-day value of a business*, many brokers and business owners tend to utilize ONLY "the multiple method" when they want a "quick and easy" way to determine a business's worth. While appraisers enter complex equations into complicated computer software to determine a business's value, brokers and owners scribble a quick multiple calculation onto the back of a napkin to try to simplify the valuation process.

THE MULTIPLE

To illustrate a calculation of value, I, too, will *over-simplify the process*. Although *this is just a piece of the puzzle* in the income approach to business valuation, we need to understand the valuation's multiple.

A business broker may calculate your business's sales price by multiplying your cash flow by an industry multiple. For instance, he could use the simple following equation:

Obviously, you understand that your BUSINESS VALUE will be its ideal list price, and I have listed EBITDA as a way of equalizing your cash flow compared to other companies within your industry, but what is the multiplying factor? Essentially, it is a numerical or percentage-based value that indicates the health of a business *in comparison to its industry peers*. To an appraiser, your multiplier will fall between the numbers one through ten along a bell curve depending on the efficiency, modernity, etc. of your business in relation to other businesses like yours. **Essentially, the multiplying factor is its health standard**.

For instance, if your EBITDA is $2 million and your industry's average multiplying factor is 4, then you could list your business for sale at $8 million.

Or if they use the percentage multiplier… your EBITDA is $2 million and your industry's average multiplying percentage is 70, then your sales price could be $1.4 million.

Simple, right? Not even close. Honestly, friends, the calculation I've just given you is an *over-simplification* of several, complex calculations business appraisers use to determine a business's value based on the money the company earns.

CONTACT AN EXPERT

By identifying and appraising your assets, you and your advisory team can come up with a rough valuation of your business. You can even enter information about your company's assets into benchmarking tools on the internet to derive a very basic value of your business. Although your team's calculations or a software program's calculations may assess your company's potential value, remember that those calculations are just an *assessment*; they are **not** a *formal estimate* of your company's value.

Almost any business owner or his professional advisors can use the company's balance sheet or Profit and Loss Statement to determine cash flow, assets, and liabilities. You can plug any number into any equation to determine what your business is worth, but can you determine whether you have used the correct number or the correct equation? You can place a subjective value on your tangible assets, but do you know the value of your intangible assets? You can list quantifiable liabilities, but can you evaluate the risks the economy, the government, the environment, or the market pose to your business's sellability?

Simple math equations and calculations do not take the place of a trained professional who has the education, the experience, and the know-how to formulate a realistic sales price based on all factors that affect your company's value. For a formal analysis of your business's current value, you will need to hire a Certified Valuation Analyst® (CVA®) or similar professional who has the education, experience, and necessary know-how, to determine a formal and realistic sales price.

These professionals realize that actual worth has more to do with the *achievable and creditable forecast* of your business's future within the economic marketplace than with your current sales, asset holdings, income, or inventory. A CVA® understands the complexities that go into value calculations and knows that "value" is a subjective term. A CVA® can calculate a business's value using one or a combination of appraisal methods and complex calculations so when you are ready for a formal appraisal, contact an expert.

CHAPTER 9

LOOK FOR MONEY LEFT ON THE TABLE

"We need to be fast like a startup, agile like a software company and innovative like no other logistics player in order for us to be an industry leader in a digitalized world."

Unknown

Recently, I heard a fellow business owner lament, "Man Justin, I'm gonna be working in my business until I die." Laughing, I said, "Dude, I hope not," but I recognized the genuine fear behind what he said, and it was legitimate. ***Ultimately, had the business he invested his blood, sweat, tears, and savings into become nothing more than a glorified job, or could he turn it into a valuable investment commodity?***

QUESTIONS TO ANSWER

Once you and your advisory team place a basic valuation on your business or once you have received a formal valuation of your business from a CVA®, you have some questions to answer.

Are you happy with that valuation? Did you believe your business was worth more than that? If it sells at its current value, will you make enough money to retire or to begin the next phase of your life? Is there a significant gap between what your company is worth and what a similar company down the road from you is worth? What accounts for that gap? Why does your business not lead or exceed your industry's market value? What areas need renovation? Do you have to list your business for sale immediately regardless of its "low" valuation, or do you have time to strengthen its weak areas?

I talk to many business owners who are starting to ponder their future retirement. They expect the income they have made in their business and the income they make from the sale of their business to fund their retirement. Many are shocked to learn that they have not saved enough money or created enough value within their business to reach their retirement goals. They now have major decisions and adjustments to make. They can either accept the business's current valuation and sell for less than they imagined, or they can make some adjustments in and to their business to increase its value.

THE VALUE GAP

Whenever I work with business owners, I want to help them increase their business's value for the day when they plan to leave it. After they receive a valuation, if there is a deficit between what they need from the business and what they will likely get from the business, or a deficit between the value of their company and the value of their industry peers' companies, many business owners think they can just go out and work harder. They 'know' they can drive up sales. They 'know' they can get more customers. More sales means higher value, right? As a lifelong entrepreneur and business owner, I certainly understand this line of thinking. However, this may not be the best approach. In fact, increasing revenue to the company could lead to a decrease in VALUE.

Let me explain. Many businesses are operating at or near capacity. Additional sales will put stress on the business in key areas. The increase of sales could cause stress on the overworked team resulting in higher team turnover, or higher absence rates… ultimately decreasing margin and driving down the VALUE of the company. Increased sales and increased workloads also drive up employee compensation and tax liabilities which increases business expenses without necessarily increasing profit margins. Thus, increasing sales could create a financial vortex that leads to a decrease in business value.

Trying to increase cash sales without planning how to strengthen your company's weaknesses will be like paddling faster on one side of a canoe; you will continue moving but you will go in circles never getting anywhere, only moving faster. If you are not careful, you will never reach your financial goals. Rather than paddling around in circles trying to increase sales alone, you need to find a way to increase your business's value to compete with industry leaders *without increasing risk to your company*. You must find another way to bridge the "value gap."

What exactly does that mean? Most simply, a value gap is the difference between your company's current value and the value of a best-in-class leading industry peer. If you are selling bottles of water, and an appraiser values your company at $10 per share, but the best-in-class water bottling company that makes similar revenue in a similar economic environment and in a similar region sells for $40 per share, then you have a value gap.

This past year, I ran into this type of situation with a client of mine who I will call Dentist Jeff. When his advisory team and I started working with Dentist Jeff, we determined that his business, "ABC Dental," was worth approximately $1 million. Yet, ABC Dental's industry peers *with similar revenue streams* were selling for approximately $4 million, not $1 million. In this scenario, then, ABC Dental had a $3 million value gap! There was room for Jeff's business to grow in value from $1 million to $4 million without creating additional revenue streams and risk.

Let me be clear. The existence of a value gap is determined through a comparison of similar companies—companies similar in revenue, product, service, region, size, team, economic climate, SIC code, etc. Internal forces cause the gap, not external forces. When Dentist Jeff wanted to sell ABC Dental, an appraiser valued his practice at $1 million. Yet, Jeff knows that "XYZ Dental" on the next street over recently sold for $3 million. Assuming Jeff and Paul, the owner of XYZ Dental, spoke about their revenue streams over lunch one day, Dentist Jeff knows that he and Paul have similar revenue streams, and obviously, they work in the same market and geographic region. Then why is Jeff's dental practice worth so much less than Paul's dental practice?

Well, Paul, whose practice sold for $3 million, practices dentistry with state-of-the art equipment. He has purchased the most technologically advanced x-ray machines, drills, autoclaves, and the like. He has equipment in-office that allows him to manufacture crowns so that he can place permanent porcelain crowns in patients' mouths the same day he preps their teeth. Additionally, he has tools, talent, and skill sets available in-office to practice forms of periodontics, orthodontics, endodontics, and oral surgery so that he does not have to refer patients to other providers. He has invested money to send his employees for additional degrees and credentials to increase his scope of service.

Not only does Paul have the best equipment available, he also uses the best materials provided within the industry. The resins he buys for composite tooth fillings may be expensive, but he saves time and money by using them because patients do not have to come back to have fillings redone. Paul also keeps his office's interior design features modern and clean. He added flat screen TVs in each examination room and in the waiting room for patient entertainment and comfort, and he added a play fort to the waiting room. Each of those additions have brought in new patients because parents feel comfortable bringing their children to his office rather than taking them to a pediatric dentist.

On the other hand, Jeff, whose practice is valued at $1 million, practices dentistry with equipment that was state of the art 20 years ago. Since he does not own equipment to manufacture crowns in-office, he must prepare a patient's tooth in one visit, send the tooth mold to a lab for manufacturing, get the patient back two to three weeks later, and seat the permanent crown at a second visit. Additionally, he does not have the tools, talent, or skill-sets available to practice periodontics, endodontics, orthodontics, or oral surgery, so he must send his patients to other providers for these specialized services.

In addition to out-of-date equipment, Jeff uses standard, mediocre materials for fillings and has the lab use those types of materials for his crowns. Sure, he saves money on initial cost of materials, but he ends up losing money because he often has to see patients multiple times to fix the same tooth because the material he used failed.

Just as Jeff skimps on materials and equipment, he skimps on the physical office. He redecorated about five years ago, but he has no children's area, no added patient conveniences, no TVs, no comforts, etc. His employees keep the office organized, but Dentist Jeff refuses to pay anyone to deep clean the office on a frequent basis, so dust and debris accumulates.

If a buyer were to look at XYZ and ABC Dental's balance sheets alone, he might appraise the practices at an identical value. However, when an appraiser goes into the offices and looks at décor, equipment, talent, services, operations, and the like, he will determine that Paul's practice is significantly more valuable than Jeff's. It is the *intrinsic value* his equipment, his staff, his services, and his conveniences offer his patients that makes the difference. That intrinsic value creates the value gap between these two companies.

THE VALUE OF THE MULTIPLE

Therefore, if or when your business does not appraise for a price comparable to leading industry peers, you have the option to make changes in your company to increase its value. To do this, you have the option to change either your company's cash flow (with its potential risks) and/or its multiple. Let's go back to our *over-simplified* valuation equations:

For the sake of example, let's have your company's current valuation look like this:

Original Business's Value

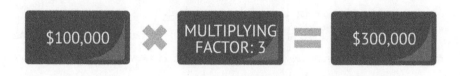

Now, let's increase company earnings OR its multiple by 25 percent:

The Business Value with a 25% increase in revenue

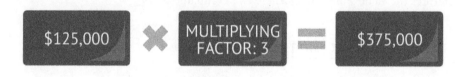

OR

The Busines Value with a 25% increase in the multiplier

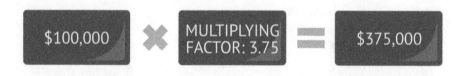

You will notice that the 25% increases to either revenue or the multiplier equated to the same increase to $375,000 valuation. Yet, remember that an increase in revenue brings an increase in risk to the company. Therefore, the value of your multiplier might actually decrease if you increase revenue alone.

In the example I gave about Dentists Jeff and Paul, their dental offices had equivalent revenue. Thus, the difference in their companies' value came down to the multiplying factor. The intrinsic value of their offices changed the value of their multipliers, not their cash flow. You see, increasing the multiplier is the key to bridging the value gap!

How, then, do you increase the multiple of your business *without* increasing your cash flow?

If appraisers recognize a range of multiples within each industry, how do you increase your multiple? How do you raise your multiple from 2 to 4 or from 70 to 85 percent? Well, if your tangible assets sell separately in an asset or market sale, and your cash flow accounts for the base value in the income valuation equation, then your **intangible assets** (the remaining form of capital) affect your multiple. Essentially, those intangible assets—employees, customers, performance, systems, culture, brand recognition, intellectual property, independence from the owner, transferability, reputation, etc.—drive up your multiple, which exponentially increases your business value.

If you decide to increase your business's value to bridge the value gap between your company and leading companies in your industry, it is time to add a Certified Value Growth Advisor (CVGA®) to your advisory team that we talked about in Chapter 2. Ideally, either the CPA or CFP® you have chosen has this valuable credential, but if neither does, you need to contact a value growth expert to help you assess and sure-up your intangible assets.

CHAPTER 10

PLAN TO INCREASE YOUR BUSINESS'S VALUE

"Position your value, not your price."

Mac Duke

B efore we get deeper into the weeds, let's make these complex ideas *financially simple.*

Here are the facts thus far:

1. To determine your business's current value in your marketplace, you can multiply your cash flow by a factoring number or percentage.

2. Industry norms set an average multiplying factor or percentage, starting at the number 1 or the percentage of 10.

3. If your EBITDA (cash flow) equals your competitors', then the multiplying factor is what makes another company worth more than your company.

4. The strength (or value) of your intangible assets increases or decreases the industry's average multiple in the business valuation equation.

THE VALUE OF INTANGIBLE ASSETS

To bridge the value gap, then, you must increase the value of your intangible assets, your company's intrinsic value. Christopher Snider, founder and CEO of the Exit Planning Institute, calls a business's intangible assets its "knowledge assets," and he proposes that in today's technologically savvy business world "wealth is created by your ability to create, transfer, assemble, integrate, protect, and exploit knowledge assets."[26]

In his book, *Walking to Destiny*, Snider explains that the value of a business's knowledge assets, or the value of its intangible assets, *multiply* a business's overall worth because "they can be bought and shared." Furthermore, Snider states that a business's **intellectual capital** (its knowledge assets/its intangible assets) can be broken into four categories—"**the Four Cs.**"

- Human Capital: The value and health of a company's employees—their expertise, their training, their experience, their know-how, their intelligence, their loyalty, their capabilities, their abilities, their skill level, their age, their dependability, their happiness, etc.

  To increase the value of your multiple to become the leader in your industry, your employees must be extraordinary in all the listed categories.

- Customer Capital: The value and health of a company's customer base—their loyalty, their locale, their income brackets, their needs and your ability to fulfill them, their diversity, etc.

  To increase the value of your multiple to become the leader in your industry, you cannot depend on one customer because that one customer may not choose to do business with a future owner. You need a diverse client base with multiple clients who can easily transition under new ownership.

- Structural Capital: The value and health of a company's systems—its management systems, its management software, its financial statements, its financial software, its Key Performance Indicators of strengths and weaknesses, etc.

  To increase the value of your multiple to become the leader in your industry, you must have clear, quantifiable financial reports that show your business's historical growth, its current condition, and its pro-

26 Snider, Christopher M. *Walking to Destiny: 11 Actions an Owner MUST Take to Rapidly Grow Value & Unlock Wealth*. (2016). ThinkTank Publishing. Cleveland, Ohio.

jected revenue. Also, the stronger your business's management systems are, the easier it will be for a new owner to transition in with little to no disruption to everyday business operations.

- Social Capital: The value and health of a company's image—its brand, its brand recognition, its reputation, its local presence, its marketability, its regional presence, its national presence, its global presence, its trademarks, its logos, etc.

To increase the value of your multiple to become the leader in your industry, you should have recognizable images attached to your company that remain untarnished by scandal or negative press. The more marketable your company is, the more valuable your commodity will be to potential buyers.

Types of Capital that Increase Business Value

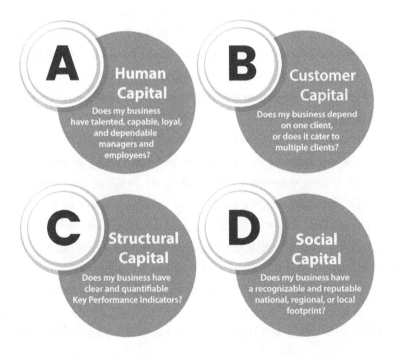

INCREASE YOUR COMPANY'S VALUE

Besides showing what kind of intellectual capital creates value in businesses, Chris Snider gives business owners an outlined plan to prepare their companies for sale. With a goal of helping business owners realize the maximum sales price for their business, he tells readers that driving up the value of their multiple will simultaneously increase their revenue. According to Snider, increased value of the multiple plus increased revenue are primary ways to increase profit during the sale of the business.

In his book, Snider coins the term "value acceleration" and defines it as a proven process that focuses on value growth through the alignment of business, personal, and financial goals.[27] In my words, *value acceleration is when business owners purposefully focus their attention on maximizing the value of their business to build it into a business that people will want to buy.*

For example, let's assume that your EBITDA is $1 million, and your current multiplying factor is 2, making your current business value $2 million. Sounds great, right? Well, what if I tell you that your industry's average multiplying factor is 4? Your multiple 2 doesn't sound as good, does it? You are leaving money on the table because your company could be worth $4 million. If you want to increase your company's value using the value acceleration methodology, your goal is to increase your multiplying factor to that industry standard of 4 or to a factor greater than 4.

As we mentioned before, our first goal is NOT to increase your revenue. *However, as you focus on increasing the intrinsic value of your company, you will likely gain more customers, clients, or patients, and more revenue will flow in.* Therefore, when a professional valuator reappraises your business after you have taken the time to increase your company's intangible asset value, he will multiply your new EBITDA of $1.5 million by a new factor of 4. That makes your company worth $6 million, not just $2 million or $4 million!

You were probably thinking I was off my rocker as you were reading the previous chapter. What type of advisor actually says, DON'T INCREASE INCOME? Seriously! I was trying to drive home this point; **if you focus on**

---

27 Snider, Christopher M. *Walking to Destiny: 11 Actions an Owner MUST Take to Rapidly Grow Value & Unlock Wealth*. (2016). ThinkTank Publishing. Cleveland, Ohio.

increasing the multiple, income will follow. As you focus on the areas of your business which are directly impacted by your intangible assets, then you free up production capacity, create efficient systems, and ultimately attract more income.

If you are not ready to sell your company, either because you have not reached that point in your life or because its valuation came back too low for your liking, you can follow the "value acceleration" methodology to identify, protect, and build your business's value. Rather than working *in* your business, you can work *on* your business by developing a systematic **growth plan**.

Your growth plan will be like your structural business plan. However, rather than focusing on defining, explaining, and quantifying every aspect of your business, **you will focus on increasing the value of your intangible assets within a specific time period**. By following four basic steps, you can increase your company's value and *maximize* your company's worth for its eventual sale.

Steps to Maximize Business Capital

REVISE THE GROWTH PLAN
- Adjust current strategies according to what's working or not working
- Create new strategies to deal with new circumstances

4

- Key employees
- Family members
- Business managers
- CERTIFIED FINANCIAL PLANNER™
- Certified Public Accountant
- Business and/or tax attorney

GATHER RELIABLE TEAM MEMBERS

1

3

REVIEW THE GROWTH PLAN REGULARLY
- Review quantifiable data with your team weekly, monthly, quarterly, and yearly
- Focus on 90 day sprints
- Assess success and failure

- Create quantifiable strategies to meet those value goals
- Focus on the 4 Cs to increase value
- Determine your business's end goals

CREATE A GROWTH PLAN AS A TEAM

2

1. First, **assemble a growth team** made up of your professional advisors, family members, key employees, board members, and managers. You want people present who can objectively listen and observe, and you want people present who are part of your day-to-day operations and life to get the most comprehensive feedback and to develop the most comprehensive strategies to accelerate value.

2. Second, **create a growth plan** as a team so that you get buy-in from all parties who can effectively bring about change within your company. Identify the strengths and weaknesses within your intangible assets, and clearly define your business's end valuation goal. Then, create systematic methods and quantifiable measurements to increase the value of your human capital, your customer capital, your structural capital, and your social capital.

3. Third, **review your growth plan** regularly so that you do not lose focus. Meet with your team weekly, monthly, quarterly, and yearly to assess your progress and quantify your results. If you have to, work on improving one intangible asset at a time. Then, evaluate how effective your strategies for improvement have been.

4. Last, **revise your growth plan** according to your quantifiable results. If you see that the value of your assets is declining rather than accelerating, you must adjust your plans to fix the problem. New risks could also arise throughout your period of growth, and you will need to revise your growth plans to meet your new business needs.

If you follow this process, the timing of your business sale becomes largely irrelevant. You can drive the business value multiplier higher weekly, monthly, quarterly, and yearly. Because you focus on growing your business's value to sell it for maximum profit, your company's value increases despite economic recession or progression.

CHARACTERISTICS VALUABLE TO THE BUYER

As you and your growth team create a plan to drive up the value of your intangible assets, you need to know what makes them attractive to potential buyers. In other words, if you are working to make your business healthy, then you must know what health looks like.

Although I could list 50-100 business attributes that attract potential buyers, I find that the following six characteristics appear near the top of every buyer's wish list:

1. Is it *profitable*? Is your business cash flow positive?

2. Is it *competitive*? Is your business beating the competition?

3. Is it *scalable*? Can your business expand or downsize quickly enough to meet demand?

4. Is it *sustainable*? Can your business withstand economic and personal storms?

5. Is it *transferable*? Can a new owner step into your business without disruptions to its day-to-day operations?

6. Is it *invulnerable*? Have you lowered all known risk factors?

If your goal at the end of business is to sell your company and live off its proceeds, then you must know what makes your company healthy and sellable. By knowing what buyers look for—profit, competitive advantage, scalability, sustainability, transferability, and invulnerability—you can create a growth plan for building and accelerating value within your intangible assets.

Increase the Value of Your Intangible Assets

"Don't be afraid to give up the good to go for the great."

John D. Rockefeller

A s you look to the eventual sale of your business, you can strategically and purposefully build value within your company by increasing
the value of your intangible assets. By strengthening your human capital,
your customer capital, your structural capital, and your social capital,
you can exponentially increase the overall sellable worth of your company. Once you increase the worth of your intellectual capital, you can use
it to make your business healthy and yourself wealthy.

CHAPTER 11

INVEST IN YOUR BENCH

"If you think it's expensive to hire a professional,
just wait until you hire an amateur."

Unknown

To increase the value of your multiplying factor to get the most money from the sale of your business, you must increase the value of your intangible capital. Yet, one of those assets stands out among the others—**human capital**.

I have owned businesses for over 20 years, and I have worked primarily with business owners over the past 15 years. In my experience, I have learned two fundamental things about building sellable businesses:

1. Business owners whose business depends solely on them or on their knowledge and abilities have no business to sell.

2. Business owners who cannot transfer skills, knowledge, and motivation to their employees cannot sell their business.

Motivational speaker and author, Zig Ziglar, sums up my experiences best; he once said, "You don't build a business. You build people, and people build the business." Your human capital makes or breaks your business's sellability. To make sure you build your bench strong enough and deep enough, I will spend more time on human capital than on the other three types of capital, so let's jump right in and figure out how to increase the worth of the first of four knowledge assets.

HOW STRONG IS YOUR BENCH?

When I hear the question, "How strong is your bench?" I immediately think of that big barrel-chested workout buff at the gym. You know the one, the one always standing around the bench talking about how much he can bench press, as if he could bench press a house.

I also think about the bench full of second-string athletes at a football, baseball, or basketball game. These strong and talented athletes are just waiting for their chance to jump into position at a moment's notice. Coaches constantly rotate players on and off the field, or on and off the bench, to showcase and preserve the strength of their overall team.

Essentially, I'm talking about the second type of bench, but this book is about business owners, not coaches or athletes, and there are not any second-string members in business. Like the members you have already chosen for your advisory "Dream Team," each player within your business must be an all-star.

The right executives, the right division heads, the right managers, and the right employees are vital to the value growth of your business. These players, or these team members, can make or break your business. If you can build an all-star team working *within* your business in addition to the Dream Team working *on* your business, you will win the proverbial championship by selling your business.

THE COST OF HIRING THE BEST

At this point, you may be thinking, "Sure, Justin, hiring talented people is a no-brainer, but what's it going to cost me? How in the world am I going to pay for the best team?"

Hiring a good team of managers and employees is probably going to cost you more than you want to spend, but in the long run, it will cost you much less than if you never make the decision to hire the best people. You may pay a professional manager 20 percent more than you expect or want to pay but if your business can grow by 25 percent, 30 percent, or 40 percent under her leadership, then your increased revenue more than pays for her great talent. Your initial sacrifice could exponentially increase your company's worth to investors.

A rookie mistake many business owners make is being cheap on the hire, but I don't think you can overpay the right team; I really don't think you can. Hear me out. When sports teams win championships, no team owner questions the players' compensation. From the least talented to the most talented, every player's performance mattered.

Money is an incredible motivator; it can motivate people to do good, and it, unfortunately, can motivate them to do evil. When I was a kid, my mom used to tell me, "You'd clean out a horse stall with a fondue fork if someone paid you enough." I agree with that! Our team members will be more motivated if we pay them what they think they are worth. If you do not think they are worth that, hedge the bet with a performance-based bonus structure. Make the hiring experience a win-win experience to keep your team motivated to perform.

If you want to build an unbelievable bench to compete in the business market, you must make the decision to do so and allocate your money accordingly. Look at hiring a team of all-stars no matter what the initial cost because all-stars win championships. Talent increases worth. Building a management team and an employee team full of winners will take time and patience but you will be rewarded in a handsome sales price for your business at the end!

RECRUITING AN ALL-STAR TEAM FOR YOUR BENCH

Where do you start, then? Sure, you see the need to find the "right" people for your business but how in the world do you make that happen? In my years of business ownership experience and in business coaching experience, I have developed a simplified system to do just that.

Identify the position, or team member, that will add the most value to your business.

As a business owner, your personal strengths tend to shine. However, your weaknesses may be just as glaring to those around you. To strengthen your weakest areas, you should look for the person who can offset and complement your particular skill set. Hire someone to fill in the holes you inevitably leave so that your customers see no weaknesses within your business.

Recruit that team member.

Once you know what position you need to fill, you want to look for that team member. Either hire an agency to conduct the talent search for you, or buck up and do it yourself. If you use an agency, decide beforehand if you want to pay a flat-rate fee for hiring services or if you want to pay on a contingency basis when you hire the agency's chosen employee. If your small business resources are too slim to allow you to hire an agency, then you must do your due diligence to check your applicants' references. You will want to review the social media profiles, conduct interviews, discuss job requirements, and agree on pay scales.

Interview multiple candidates.

Choose several people whose qualifications fit your job requirements. Then, let them fulfill the job they will be doing so that you can compare their skill levels for specific tasks. In their working interview, give them time to mess up to see if they can acknowledge their weaknesses and make corrections. I, personally, will always choose an employee with good character over an employee with impressive skills. Skills can be taught and improved; character and personality cannot.

Seek legal counsel.

Now is the time you need to rely on that amazing business attorney on your advisory Dream Team. You want to tell your lawyer your hiring goals and get help with employment negotiations and contract implementations. I believe that you should always work with someone who has your best interest at heart and who knows how to protect you and your business.

Once you master the hiring process, whether you go through an agency or hire the individual yourself, you will repeat it until you have built out your entire management and employee team. Yes, I said "team." You cannot stop after hiring one person. You want to fill your bench with all-star team members because, ultimately, you want this business to operate autonomously without you, the founder, the Grand Poobah.

You are not going to win a championship right away. Your business will not sell for millions now, but if you plan ahead, you can win that business championship. You can stack your bench with the right people who will buy-in to your business plan and your business growth plan. They will know how to implement the best management systems which will help your business expand and become scalable which will ultimately increase your company's sellable value.

CHAPTER 12

ENCOURAGE TEAM MEMBER LOYALTY

"Essentially, having terms and conditions protects you as a business. Terms and conditions certainly have an important role to play when it comes to two parties understanding their duties, rights, roles, and responsibilities."

Emma Jones

HELP NOT WANTED

I shared a "Help Wanted" post on my Facebook feed some time ago, searching for the right team member to fill an executive position in my company. Sure enough, one of my friends gave me the name of a candidate who seemed to fit the position profile. During an interview, I asked this candidate, "Where do you see yourself in a couple of years?" I'll never forget his reply. With no shame, the young man said, "You know, I've always wanted to start my own business. I thought working with you would give me enough information to go out and start my own business one day."

Now as a business owner, that is an instant, "no-hire," but I was intrigued, so I asked him, "What type of business are you thinking about starting?" He answered, "A wealth management firm kinda like yours. I want to work with small business owners like you do." At this point, I'm thinking, "Are you serious?!?! You want me to hire you so I can teach you how to go out and become my competition? Yeah, right. I was born at night, just not last night, buddy."

91

THE ALLURE OF GREENER PASTURES

Why should I invest all my time, energy, and money training and equipping another company's employee? That's crazy!

However, if you train your team members and they leave to be a part of a competitor's workforce or to become your competition, then you are doing just what I would have done if I had hired that job candidate. How ludicrous would it be to give your competitors your best employees and the knowledge they have gained from you? Yet, so many businesses lose good, quality team members to their competition. According to Emily Bonnie, a researcher and writer for a work management web-based platform, employee turnover costs US companies $160 billion a year.[28]

Even if you offer employee benefits and treat your employees well, competing companies might lure your team members away with promises of greener grass. Sometimes, you must gently prod your employees back in the right direction with "sticks" of liability protection for yourself. With company-specific protective agreements, you can reinforce team member loyalty and protect yourself from harm. The protective agreements can also clarify employee/employer expectations at hiring time.

EMPLOYEE AGREEMENTS CAN HELP "ENCOURAGE" LOYALTY

If your competitors do happen to catch your employees' eyes, what can you do to guide your team members gently back to your company? A healthy fear of ramifications can lead your team members in the right direction at the beginning of your working relationship or it can guide them back to you if they stray.

What exactly does that mean? What agreements or restrictions can you put in place to keep your employees from becoming your competition or from going to competing companies?

---

28 Boone, Emily. Employee Retention: The True Cost of Losing Your Best Talent. (April 2017). Retrieved from https://www.wrike.com/blog/employee-retention-true-cost-losing-best-talent/

- A Non-Compete Agreement keeps your employees from working with or as your competition for a designated period of time.

- Non-Solicit Agreements prevent your employees from soliciting customers and employees away from you, and they prevent vendors from soliciting your employees.

- A Confidentiality Agreement keeps employees from revealing company secrets if they leave or talk to other business owners.

- Intellectual Property Agreements keep work employees did for a company within that company if the employee leaves.

Friends, most business owners want to build a dedicated team of employees who have their best interests at heart, and there is a fine line between making employees fearful and establishing healthy protections against employee retribution or employee turnover. Before enforcing any employee agreements, consult with your advisory attorney to protect yourself from any known or unknown business risks. Not all court jurisdictions honor employer-employee agreements, so check with a professional before you implement any of them to be sure they protect you.

CHAPTER 13

CULTIVATE A CULTURE OF KINDNESS

*"You don't build a business. You build people,
and then people build the business."*

Zig Ziglar

CAN I "HELP" YOU?

My dad and I were in the middle of one of our multi-weekend hunting trips a few years back. Each morning, before heading into the woods, we would pull up to a particular fast food restaurant, and Dad would order a sausage biscuit. When he got down the road a bit and went to eat his biscuit, he would realize he had the wrong order. Now, my dad was a pretty easy-going, pretty happy-go-lucky guy most of the time, so instead of getting mad, he would say, "Welp, I guess I'm gonna eat a bacon, egg, and cheese biscuit today." After three weekends in a row of getting the wrong order, the situation got downright funny.

The last weekend we made this hunting trip, Dad pulled up to the restaurant's order box and recognized the voice of the young girl who had taken his order the last three weeks. When she asked him how she could help him, Dad very courteously said, "I'll tell you what. You just pick out any biscuit you wanna give me and charge me for it. I'm good." We pulled around, chuckling to ourselves. We weren't trying to make a stink; the situation was just funny. We definitely were NOT getting top-notch service.

EMPLOYEE MOTIVATION MATTERS

Everyone has been to a business and been shrugged off by an uncaring employee. We have all seen the dark side of business customer service. Employee turnover and employee unhappiness or inefficiency can hurt a company's value from the buyer's perspective. If a buyer notices that your current employees do not want to be at work or that your best employees have already left, why would they want to buy your business? If they do decide to buy, they would probably offer you less than top market value for your business.

Creating a business in which employees feel valued, challenged, and inspired can help bring you top dollar when you go to sell your business. Business buyers, as well as customers, recognize the difference between vibrant, happy employees and discontent, unmotivated employees, and they recognize the value happy, motivated team members bring to the business.

CULTIVATE A CULTURE OF KINDNESS

I have worked with hundreds of business owners over the years, and most of those owners want to talk about money or the problems they have with employees. They talk about how they want to attract more customers or gain more market share; yet, I can count on one hand how many business owners have talked to me about building a mutually respectful business relationship with employees. Sure, they want to talk about owner-employee relations, but they complain about poor employee work ethic or disrespectful employees rather than asking me how to add value to their team or how to improve employee morale. They tend to focus on their own grievances rather than on how to rectify employee grievances, and they prefer to play the martyr rather than work to rebuild owner-employee relations.

Although this goes without saying, I want to remind you that people are not objects. Business owners, especially, should not follow the meta-narrative of our nation's self-serving culture. Instead, you should cultivate a culture of kindness in your company where values like respect, trust, and fairness lay the groundwork for owner-employee relations. Employees who feel appreciated, valued, well compensated, and respected will most likely provide respectful and courteous service to your customers. Therefore, I believe that everything in our business blooms out of our values.

If value is where everything blooms, then culture is where everything grows.

Using agrarian terms, let me put it this way. Values are akin to the soil in which we plant our seeds of kindness and respect. If the soil is good, then the seeds should germinate and yield the flowers we want them to produce. That is value.

Culture is like the macro-environment, or the climate-controlled greenhouse. If the soil is good but the environment is not conducive to growth, chances are the seeds will not germinate in the soil. In other words, no one plants seed in Antarctica and expects flowers to bloom even if the soil is "good." Both the soil and its environment must be solid.

Growing flowers is like growing a business to sell. You want to build a business that exudes values and culture buyers want and customers expect. Your life's worth is at stake here. If you have poor values or cannot create nurturing owner-employee relations, you will get in the employee weeds, so to speak. Your good employees will leave quicker than you can hire new ones, and your customers will realize your business has problems. Don't spend your time weeding through in-fighting and hurt feelings. Instead, cultivate an environment of harmony and hard work.

GUARD AGAINST DANGERS

While you are cultivating this harmonious environment of owner-employee respect and loyalty, you should be on your guard against known dangers to your company's "greenhouse." If you do not guard against the following dangers, you could lose the team members you have worked so hard to get. High employee turnover will expose your company's poor values and disdainful culture, and buyers will sense the tension in your owner-employee relationships.

Avoid Lip Service

If your website tells customers that you value open communication and employee loyalty, but you scan through emails on your phone when your team members voice ideas, what good does that do? If your walk does not match your talk, you are probably going to lose good team members and customers. It really is that simple, folks.

Don't Get Greedy

If "Super Star Steve" sells more products in a day than any of your other employees sell in a week but you give him the same commission that you give "Lazy Larry," how motivating is this to Larry? How long will Steve continue to work that hard? Owner greed demotivates employees when it denies them higher incentivized compensation for bonuses.

Get Help

Business owners are often great at many things, but building company-wide morale may not be one of your strengths. If you struggle with the ins and outs of owner-employee relations, do not be afraid to hire a Human Resource (HR) advisor or an on-site HR team member.

At some point in the future, a buyer will look into the heart of this company you are planning to sell, and he will recognize your values and the type of culture you promote within your business. A company with strong values and a kind culture, one that promotes strong owner-employee relations, will bring more money and more reward than a company with poor values and a spiteful culture.

Have fun in your business. Love what you do, but create a culture within your business where your employees can love what they do, too.

CHAPTER 14

REWARD YOUR TEAM

"We rise by lifting others."

Robert Ingersoll

Owner-employee relations tend to expose a company's core values, so how do we cultivate or build positive values within our company? I believe that if you take care of your employees, your team members, they will take care of you, your company, and your customers. As J.W. "Bill" Marriott once said, "If you take care of your employees, they will take care of your customers, and your business will take care of itself." Creating employee incentive programs can enhance happiness within and employee loyalty to your company.

MY SUCCESS IS YOUR SUCCESS

Years ago, a company recruited a friend of mine to grow its small business into a multimillion-dollar business within a short period of time. When the owner hired Chris, the owner promised him shared income and incentives. He said, "Look, we're gonna share in the company. Your success as a team member is going to be my success as the owner. My success as the owner is going to be your success as a team member."

Long story short, my friend took that company from $10 million to more than $300 million in revenue within that timeframe, and when the owner sold the business, he followed through on his promise and provided my friend with the biggest paycheck he had ever received. Chris called it a "life-changing check." When he wrote about that payday in his book, *Walking to Destiny,* my friend Christopher Snider said, "Man this [check] changed my life. This is what changes legacies for families."[29]

I often ask myself and clients I work with, "How can we build a team dedicated to helping us reach our goal to sell the business?" If you have a stable bench of team players who help you realize profit within your business when you sell it, more than likely, you will want to be philanthropic. You will want to show benevolence towards those individuals who are in the dirt and the grime, pulling towards the goal with you, but before you "give away the farm," you should look at strategies you can implement to incentivize employees and still have your desired payout upon the sale of your business.

As you look at types of incentives to offer your employees, keep in mind the following rules:

- Give all team members a way to piggyback on your company's financial success.

- Have continencies in place to ensure the commitment of your management team if a buyer requires their expertise.

- Reward team members for actions you want to encourage.

LONG-TERM EMPLOYEE INCENTIVE PROGRAMS

If you want to be benevolent and fair, one way to incentivize team members over the long-term course of their employment is to offer them a stock option. I will spend time in a later chapter detailing the stock option, but at this point, my goal is just to introduce you to the idea at its highest level. I will tell you, though, that if you are going to entertain the idea of a stock-option plan or stock options for your company, then you want to have a competent attorney and a power-house accountant on your professional advisory team. There are plenty of red-tape barriers and legal risks surrounding stock options, so you will need a good consulting team.

29 Snider, Christopher M. *Walking to Destiny: 11 Actions an Owner MUST Take to Rapidly Grow Value & Unlock Wealth*. (2016). Think Tank Publishing House. Cleveland, Ohio.

The Employee Stock Ownership Plan (the ESOP)

At its simplest, a stock-option plan is an organized retirement account held by a trustee for the benefit of your company's employees. Cincinnati-based attorney and fellow Certified Exit Planning Advisor (CEPA), Ben Wells, specializes in employee stock options, and he explains that while employees can *purchase* company stocks, or ownership shares, through the retirement plan, they do not have a right to vote the shares. Neither do they get to elect the board of directors or say how the company should be run. However, when they retire, they receive payment based on what the shares are worth at that time.[30]

I believe that if you can get an employee to invest the money he earns into the very company for which he works, then you have a dedicated employee; you have someone who sees value in your business and puts his dollars to work within it. As Jesus says in Matthew 6:21, "For where your treasure is, there will your heart be also."

The Phantom Stock Option

What do you do, though, if you want to reward employees but you do not want to give up stock in your company? Well, another way to offer long-term employee incentives is through phantom stock, or what's called stock appreciation rights. In this method, you provide money to employees without ceding ownership or control.

Within a phantom stock option, you can create a bonus structure for key employees that pays them based on a "phantom," or figurative ownership, share in your company. So while you own 100 percent of the stock in your corporation or LLC, you can pay your employees an ownership percentage when your company does well. That way, your employees do not get all up in your business, so to speak, but they stay motivated and dedicated to your end goals.

---

30 Goodbread, Justin (Writer, Producer, and Interviewer), & Wells, Ben (Interviewee). (2018). ESOPS: An In-Depth Look at a Way to Sell Your Business to Employees. Retrieved from https://financiallysimple.com/should-you-sell-your-business-to-employees-pros-and-cons-of-esops/

SHORT-TERM EMPLOYEE INCENTIVE PROGRAMS

Not all employees see a long-term reward as a reason to stay at a place of employment. Business owners should probably offer "sweet treats" along the way. Short-term employee incentive plans can keep your team members happy and motivated so they don't look for positions at competing companies. Remember, you do not want to train your employees to work for or to become your competition. Positive reinforcement and instant gratification can work like a carrot held out on a stick does for a donkey. Short-term employee incentives can also foster team member harmony and cohesion.

Then, what types of things might motivate employees?

- Recognition – If an employee does a good job, reward him openly with verbal praise. A simple "thank you" or "good job" can make almost anyone feel appreciated, wanted, and needed.

- Fringe Benefits – Healthcare benefits, 401(k) matches, and the like can set your company above your competitor's in the eyes of employees.

- Paid Time Off – The opportunity for earned and compensated time off adds value to your employee workplace.

- Annual Bonuses – Merited or unmerited, a Christmas bonus or a work anniversary bonus can add to employee happiness and commitment to your company.

- Production Based Rewards – Employees can become extremely motivated to work hard if they know they can earn trips to desirable locations, monetary bonuses, redeemable merchant gift cards, or many other types of gifts.

- Peace and Happiness – Incentives do not always come in time, gifts, or money. Simply creating a respectful and happy work environment can create employee loyalty for years to come.

Whichever way you decide to incentivize employees, make sure you have a good lawyer and an amazing accountant to guide you. You will need help wading through the rights, warrants, risks, and taxes that come with stock ownership, stock options, fringe benefits, paid time off, bonuses, and gifts, but let me give you a word of caution—don't go to your next team meeting and mention that you are considering incentives until you have talked to your advisory team. You should not blindly offer something you may ultimately find too risky. Additionally, you don't want to offer your employee incentive programs without educating employees about the guidelines and requirements involved.

Employee incentives can help your employees catch your vision to grow and sell your business. Financial gain can motivate owners *and* employees, so rewarding every member of your team, from the maintenance man to the CEO, can build the value of your team and consequently the company when you are ready to sell it.

CHAPTER 15

EXPAND AND DIVERSIFY YOUR CUSTOMER BASE

*"There's a big difference between a satisfied customer
and a loyal customer. Never settle for 'satisfied.'"*

Shep Hyken

B y directly taking care of your employees, you indirectly take care of your customers. Author and marketing expert, Sybil Stershic, explains this phenomenon well by stating, "The way your employees feel is the way your customers will feel. And if your employees don't feel valued, neither will your customers."[31] What you should begin to see here is that each of the four Cs of intangible capital affects the others.

Strengthening your human capital can increase your customer capital. If employees are happy, they can make customers happy. Satisfied customers become loyal customers. Loyal customers bring in more customers. More customers challenge you to increase your product or service lines to meet new customers' needs.

Once you increase your customer and product bases, you will need to expand your social capital by marketing so that your marketplace knows you have new products and services. While you are increasing your customer base, your sales, your services, and your influence, you will also need to strengthen your structural capital so that you can keep up with customer and sales data. Thus, as you raise the value of one form of capital, each of the other three is advantageously affected, ultimately increasing the value of your business.

---

31 Stershic, Sybil F. (2007). Taking Care of the People Who Matter Most: A Guide to Employee-Customer Care.

However, you cannot work on one form of capital and expect the other three to rise exponentially on their own. Working hard to increase the value of one "C" *can* increase the value of the others, but you also have to put some effort into each of the other "Capital Cs" to increase the overall value of your company. Therefore, let's work on improving your customer capital.

A MAJORITY HOLD

A few years ago, the owner of a marketing firm, who I'll call "Steve," called me up and asked me to help him sell his company. Since I had never worked with him before, I asked Steve to meet me for lunch to go over his company's facts and figures. While we were eating pizza (because a good pizza is needed in any business conversation), I was pouring over his business's financial reports, and what impressed me most was his rising revenue. I frequently see successful businesses increase their revenue a few percentage points each year, but I was surprised by the large gains this company was making within a relatively short period of time.

When I asked Steve about the increasing revenue, he puffed up his chest and said, "Well, Justin, that's why I want to sell. I figure that my company has to be worth a lot of money if I'm bringing in that much cash! Now's the time to get out—when buyers want what I've got."

Not one to be sidetracked, I steered Steve back to why his revenue was increasing. "Dude, I get that," I said, "but what's driving that increase in revenue? Why have your sales grown by 30 percent in one year when you've only increased sales by an average of three to five percent over the previous 15 years?"

"That's easy to explain," he boasted. "I landed a huge contract with a huge client! He gives me so much work that I hardly need any other clients. I've given most of my smaller contracts to other marketing firms so that I can devote my attention to the client who's giving me all this business!"

"Hold on a minute, hero. I think we have a problem."

WHY DIVERSIFYING CUSTOMER CAPITAL MATTERS

Come to find out, my lunch companion had a client, not a business. When I dug into his vendor lists and details, I discovered that his "huge client" provided over 80 percent of his current revenue stream, and thus, Steve had major problems. While he thought he had reached the pinnacle of success, he had cut off an arm to save a leg, so to speak.

By neglecting multiple customers, Steve lost many while he retained one. While that one provided him with a steady income, what would happen if that "one" left? That one hired him because of who he was, not because of who his company was. The client had known him for 20 years or more and trusted him as a person, so he gave the business owner all his marketing and advertising work.

What if the client became disgruntled with Steve? What if Steve sold his business to a buyer the client didn't know? Would the client stay? If the client valued Steve's hard work and long-term relationships, then he probably wouldn't give his work to an unknown buyer. That means that any buyer would immediately lose 80 percent of this company's revenue stream. Who would put himself in that situation? No one.

By focusing on one customer, Steve lost most of his other customers. That decrease in customer base and diversity ended up making him a "slave" to one company. What happened if that one customer decided to work with a different marketing firm? Steve would be left destitute, scrambling to find other clients and more work.

Steve also stopped developing new services and products since he was focusing on one customer's needs, so he limited his product base and diversity. By restricting his customers, his products, and his services, he lost the ability to grow, expand, or sustain his current income if the "huge client" took his business elsewhere. Rather than adding value to his business, Steve decreased his company's value. Essentially, he had made his business unsellable.

Maintaining customers and acquiring new customers is vital to a business's success but notice that I said "customers" not "a large customer." Adding height and depth to your customer pool allows you to swim freely within the waters of scalability, sustainability, and sellability.

EXPAND YOUR CUSTOMER CAPITAL

To expand your customer pool, you must purposefully and systematically collect data about your current customers and their purchases through a Customer Relationship Management (CRM) system, through a Point of Sale (POS) system, through your own research, or through paid data collection. Ideally, you want to know your customers' ages, spending habits, location, economic status, political status, family status, and more. You also want to know how many customers you have and how many of them return.

Knowing the information, though, is only half of the battle. You must know what to do with the data after you collect it and analyze it. Essentially, if you understand the data, you can do four things:

1. **Penetrate and saturate your existing market.**

    Once you know who your customers are, what they are buying from your company, where they live, and what their email address is, you can advertise pointedly to them. Maybe you mail or email them coupons for products they purchase most often or for products you need to liquidate. If most of your customers live in a certain zip code radius, saturate those neighborhoods and communities with promotional flyers, geofencing, business cards, or signage. Additionally, if most of the residents within that zip code match a certain age or socioeconomic demographic, try sending them appropriate promotional items bearing your business name and logo.

    For customers who frequent your business, launch a loyalty or rewards program to incentivize customers to buy from you or to refer other customers to you. Take another look at your logo and branding. Is it outdated, too simple, or too busy? Maybe you need to revitalize your logo to make it more modern, more recognizable, or more eye-catching to your customers. Think of Nike's swoosh or Target's bullseye. Then, try relaunching existing products or services with your new brand name, logo, and packaging. Focusing your advertising attention on existing customers and existing products can spark renewed interest in your business, increase current customer loyalty, or regain customers you had lost to competitors.

2. **Expand your market.**

As you increase your current customers' happiness and loyalty to your company, you create an avenue to reach new customers and to expand your reach within your marketplace. Existing customers can be your greatest source of referrals for new clients or customers because if they are happy with your services, brand, quality, products, etc., they will draw in new, unreached clients of similar demographic and geographic areas—your target market. Essentially, you keep existing clients AND reach new clients when you advertise to current customers.

However, you cannot depend solely on word of mouth to draw in new customers. If you watch any TV commercials or are aware of advertising mediums in your area, you know that Apple and Samsung do not rely on word of mouth to attract new customers. They invest marketing dollars to target new customers within their existing market niche and to search for "ideal" customers beyond their geographic and demographic marketplace.

You can do the same thing. Review the data from your CRM system again. Can you determine your customers' average age? Are they old or young? Are they single or married? Do they have children? Are they shopping for their children? What are their specific needs? What brings them to your store or facility?

If you blindly advertise to a generic group of people, you will spend your marketing dollars in vain. Whereas, if you advertise directly to a certain age group, a certain gender, a certain type of family, a certain type of parent, a certain type of professional, and the like, you are more likely to see a return on your investment. Maybe you have determined an older generational demographic makes up most of your customer base, and you're worried that you will lose your business as your customers move into nursing homes or pass away. You then identify your need for younger customers, and you advertise directly to them via new media platforms.

Reach out to new, "ideal," customers on social media. Speak to your targeted audience through radio ads or on television commercials. Speak at events your types of customers attend. Create a website that speaks to your ideal consumer, and begin online sales to reach a larger geographic marketplace. Ultimately, engage in social media campaigns with your target customer to diversify and expand your existing customer concentration.

3. **Improve your products for your existing market.**

Rebranding and advertising your products can help you instill loyalty and excitement within existing markets and launch your business into previously untapped markets, but you may also have to improve or adapt your existing products as well. New packaging can only get you so far. An inferior product in a superior package is still an inferior product. Yes, it may *look* fancier, but customers will see through the façade.

To increase your customer capital—your customer loyalty and diversity—you need to improve your product line, improve the look of your product, improve the look of your store, and improve the access customers have to your products. Maybe you should carry name brands rather than generic brands, or you should order better quality generic products. Perhaps you rearrange your products or your store to increase your products' aesthetic appeal and to make your products easier to find. Do you need to reorganize your product placements? Do you have like products placed near each other?

If you offer services rather than products, do customers know what you offer? Make sure you have an up-to-date listing of your services and fees that's visible, accessible, and easy to read. Are you upselling products with your services? Are you offering the most innovative technological services and products? Are you adapting your own products and systems to match your customers' ever-changing technological needs?

By improving your products and services and by improving your presentations of each, you can retain customers and gain new ones. However, do not pay so much attention to quality that you forget to provide excellent service or fair pricing.

Additionally, do not forget to adapt your products to keep up with market trends. Take Kodak Company, for instance. Created in the late 1800s, Kodak led the film photography industry throughout the twentieth century. Yet, when leadership saw market demand change from film to digital photography, Kodak didn't adapt and offer digital photography, even though one of its engineers created the technology! Kodak's customers embraced digital photography, and they took their business to companies who provided that, leaving Kodak in bankruptcy and ruin. Learn from that real-world example and keep your market research up-to-date so that you can adapt your products to meet changing customer needs and wants.

4.   **Diversify your products to reach new markets.**

If you are trying to tap into new markets, you can create new products or offer new services based on the demographics of your current markets. Let's look at 3M for this example. Originally known as the Minnesota Mining and Manufacturing Company, 3M became an internationally recognized and publicly traded company by expanding its reach into the fields of industry, retail, and healthcare. When its original mining trade failed to produce quality products or loyal customers, Minnesota Mining leadership encouraged their workers to design and create new products that customers *would* buy.[32] You may even recognize products 3M has developed, namely Scotch Brand Tape and Post-it notes. 3M's ability to create new products for new markets led to its continued and continuous success while other com-

---

32 Wikipedia. (August 4, 2018). 3M. Retrieved from https://en.wikipedia.org/wiki/3M

panies like Kodak, who could not or did not develop innovative new products, became relics of a past generation.

Finally, you should create new products or design new services based on the demographics of your "ideal" customers, not just your current markets. If you sell hearing aids, and most of your customers are older, but you need to attract younger customers or other businesses to grow and expand your business, what can you do? Can you use the technology you developed for your hearing aids to create other types of sound-enhancing products for use in radios, speakers, theaters, etc.? Think big, and use your human capital to help you diversify your customer capital.

As you diversify and expand your customer base, you will have to diversify and expand your products and services to keep up with demand, but increased demand brings increased risk in your business. The more markets you reach, the more politics, environmental factors, social trends, and technological advances affect your customers and thus affect your sales. Therefore, you must rely on your human capital, your structural capital, and your social capital to remain a stronghold within your industry no matter what may come.

CHAPTER 16

UPDATE YOUR SYSTEMS

"Organize around business functions, not people. Build systems within each business function. Let systems run the business and people run the systems. People come and go, but the systems remain constant."

Michael Gerber

To accelerate the value of your business, you cannot merely concentrate on the aptitude and happiness of your team members and the diversity of your customer and product bases. You must also work to increase the value and integrity of your systems, your structural capital. Ultimately, creating, updating, and/or implementing various systems within your company streamlines your processes and reports which allows the business to operate without you, the owner. As you will see in Chapter 26, the ability to transfer operational duties to your employees is vital for a seamless transition between business seller and business buyer which makes your business more attractive to potential buyers.

DOODLES ON A NAPKIN

About four years ago, a client who I will call "Frank" reached out to me for help. He had built a super successful business from the ground up, providing him approximately $1 million of take-home pay per year, and he was looking at selling the business.

To get a better understanding of Frank's business, I met him at his home way back in the country sticks and rode around to job sites with him. While we were riding around the backwoods, I asked him several questions about his business. When I asked him how he reached that $1 million income level of success, all he could tell me was that he had worked hard. Well, working hard is not an answer a buyer can quantify or qualify so I asked to see his business financial statements.

At that point, Frank got quiet. I could hear crickets; you know? To beat all, this ole country boy looked at me and said, "Well, geez Son. I run my business on the back of a napkin." "What!?!" I asked. Then, he literally opened the center console of the truck, and low and behold, he pulled out a napkin with the day's figures on it. It was hysterical!

I couldn't say much because his method yielded him unbelievable success. That was undeniable, but the method was going to turn away potential buyers because a buyer cannot take figures scribbled on a napkin to the bank. Buyers would not look at that napkin and say, "Is this a viable business for me to buy? Is this business going to be profitable for me a couple of years from now?"

For two whole years, I tried to get Frank to implement systems in his business that could make it more viable to potential buyers. After he finally "yielded" to my requests, his business experienced unbelievable growth for two years, and we were in a position to sell his company.

Now, we cannot attribute all of Frank's business growth to the systems I recommended he put in place. Some of his success had to do with economics, and some of it had to do with who he is himself. Many things contributed to his company's success, but the methods he put in place did produce quantifiable data that showed potential buyers Frank's historical growth and the company's potential future. Ultimately, Frank did sell his business.

INSTITUTE VERSATILE MANAGEMENT SYSTEMS

Deep-rooted systems that account for your structural capital help maximize your business growth so that you can make as much money as possible while minimizing growing pains and risks. You want to have a detailed, workable system implemented within every area of your business to streamline performance, to replicate tasks if you open a franchise, and to train employees quickly and efficiently. These systems usually come in the form of computer software programs, internal systems, workflow processes, management teams within your company, or consulting teams outside of your company.

Notably, I have identified nine management systems within my own companies that have dramatically increased company efficiency.

#1 – Operational Management System

First and foremost, your operating system manages all other systems. It is the written documentation of how your company runs. Whether it is a basic handwritten bubble graph on a yellow legal pad or a complicated programmed and editable flow chart, this outline details the systems you have put into place, who manages them, how they function, and the benefit they provide your company. This operational system is *the* way you can manage the company without being physically in the company.

If you have an operating system to manage all other systems effectively, you can make your structural capital the backbone of all other forms of capital—human, customer, and social.

#2 – Customer Relationship Management System (CRM) System

To obtain customers and to keep them in your business, you should put a system in place that analyzes and manages your interactions with customers. This software, or this team, will collect data about your customers that includes their demographic information, what brought them to your business, what they are buying from you, and how often they use you. The data alone does not do anything for your business, though. You must have a team or a software program that can analyze the data with the goal of improving business relationships with customers, retaining customers, and upselling to customers. Thus, you are using your structural capital to grow your customer capital.

#3 – Requests for Proposals (RFPs) System

Next, you should have a multi-step process in place to handle quotes and estimates. To avoid losing potential customers after they call for product or service quotes, you need a system in place to follow up with your prospects. Determine who will receive the Request for Proposals and who will process them. Identify which department will workup an estimate. Then, develop a formulaic process to figure estimates and institute a company-wide deadline for delivering the estimates. Ensure that the estimates get to sales people who can communicate with the potential customers and close the deal. If your process works seamlessly, and you communicate quickly and efficiently with potential customers, you will positively affect how customers feel about your company, thus increasing the value of your social capital.

#4 – Sales Management System

In this fourth system, you will need a team who knows how to use the data you collect from your CRM system and your RFP system to make potential customers actual customers. Commonly referred to as a sales funnel in the business world, this system funnels clients from the wide "prospective client" mouth of the funnel to the narrow "actual client" part of the funnel to make the sale. If your sales people follow a systematic approach to prospective client communication, your company is more likely to gain customers which increases your customer capital.

#5 – Marketing Management System

This fifth system helps you reach new customers and encourage loyalty in existing customers. Once you review the demographics of your target market from your CRM, you can plan what type of media you need to use to reach customers. Should you offer your products and services through social media, print advertising, radio announcements, or TV commercials? Have a program or team in place that can strategically get your product in front of your ideal customer.

Obviously, your human capital and structural capital increase the worth of your customer capital within this marketing system, but you are also increasing your social capital as you get your name, services, and products in front of actual and potential customers.

#6 – Research and Development Management System

As your sales and marketing systems improve, you will need a process in place to analyze the effectiveness of your products, services, and systems. Essentially, a team will identify and analyze (research) what works and what doesn't work. Then, team members will develop ways to fix issues or resolve problems, systematically eliminating company weaknesses. Team members should also work to create new or enhance existing products, services, and systems based on what is working well for your company to increase your strengths. Your goal is to eliminate weaknesses and uphold strengths to increase the health all four types of capital.

7 – Talent Management System

Usually called an "Employee Management System," this system is how you find, hire, manage, retain, and train talented people. Without a good team in place, you will not be able to reach your business goals. You want to recruit good people purposefully and methodically rather than looking for them on the spur of the moment, and then, you want to invest time into training them using your current systems.

This piece of structural capital directly affects the quality and talent of your human capital which in turn helps increase your customer, structural, and social capital.

#8 – Legal Management System

Ultimately, your business may delegate the operations of this system to a law firm as you grow, but initially, you will need a computer program or paper filing system in place to store your business agreements, contracts, correspondence, identifying information, tax records, and employment records. However, you cannot just use the system for storage. You must have a team in place who can stay up-to-date and compliant with ongoing legal changes on local, state, and federal levels.

Yet again, your human capital and your structural capital increases the worth of your business because within this system, your team identifies and collects documents you will need to build a strong appendix for your business plan.

#9 – Financial Management System

Finally, you need a system to track where your money is coming from and where it is going. Basically, this is your recordkeeping system for income and expenses, for sales and services, for products and inventory. Some financial management systems have sister CRM systems that link and sync information. Other financial management software systems have CRM components built into their basic structure so that business owners can use one program to accomplish two tasks.

This management system continues to build your structural capital by providing you with strong financial management and reporting systems that potential buyers will want in the future.

SYSTEMS ENHANCE OPERATIONS

Ultimately, you need to establish processes and systems in every area of your business. Each works like a cog in a machine, and you want to keep each well-oiled so that the machine runs smoothly, without kinks. Having clearly defined, well-oiled operational systems in place also allows the organization to operate without you, the owner. That's the idea behind systems. Every aspect of the business should be able to operate without one single person. Teach multiple people how to operate the systems you put in place, and your organization will work systematically with or without you. The organization's independence from the owner makes it an ideal investment for a future buyer because that person will have the option to invest money without investing time.

CHAPTER 17

GENERATE REPORTS FROM YOUR SYSTEMS

"Consider three important system principles: 1) You don't get what you expect. You get what you inspect. 2) When you deal in generalities, you will never have success; but when you deal in specifics, you will rarely have a failure. 3) When performance is measured, performance improves. When performance is measured and reported, the rate of improvement accelerates."

Thomas S. Monson

E stablishing systems in your business is helpful but for you to increase the value of your systems, you must implement them and use them continuously. Practice and perfect them. The more you use your systems, the more data you can collect about customers, sales, marketing techniques, products, finances, legal issues, etc. You can then generate reports from the data you collect to identify the strengths and expose the weaknesses of your business.

THE IMPORTANCE OF KEY PERFORMANCE INDICATORS

Obviously, doodles on a napkin will not satisfy potential buyers' requests for company data and reports. For buyers to observe the success (or lack of success) of your structural capital, they need to see quantifiable Key Performance Indicators (KPIs) generated by your processes and systems. More than likely, your software systems can generate these types of reports, but you must be savvy enough to interpret the information in the reports and use it to predict your performance in the future.

The difficult part of KPIs is that every business has different performance indicators. For example, dentists can predict income by pointing to the number of patients scheduled each week or to the number of patients prescheduled for the upcoming year. CERTIFIED FINANCIAL PLANNERS™, on the other hand, can look at the gross client assets they manage to determine their potential income. In a different industry, a general contractor can predict his future income, or performance, by how many signed contracts he has.

KPIs are not important for tracking income alone. They identify upcoming expenses, growth pains, risks, rewards, and opportunities. They expose product defects or employee errors. **Essentially, KPIs paint a picture of the strengths and weaknesses of your business**.

LOOK FOR KPIS WITHIN YOUR COMPANY'S REPORTS

Although every industry has different Key Performance Indicators, all businesses can generate certain types of reports that will expose their companies' strengths and weaknesses.

FINANCIAL REPORTS

Typically, business owners and buyers alike are most interested in a company's financial reports that can be generated from certain software systems. Whether you use QuickBooks™, Quicken®, Sage, Microsoft® Excel Spreadsheets, Point of Sale (POS) systems, or an outsourced bookkeeper, the accounting systems you use need to be able to compute at least two different financial reports—a balance sheet and an operating statement.

Your Certified Public Accountant has most likely asked you to print your company's balance sheet at the end of each year to begin preparing your taxes, but what exactly does it show? Very simply, the balance sheet tracks your company's assets and liabilities. It provides banks, buyers, or tax advisors a picture of what you own and what you owe.

The balance sheet provides the following information about your company:

- Net Worth - Accomplished by subtracting your liabilities from your tangible assets.

- Debt to Income Ratio - Calculated by looking at the amount of money you have borrowed compared to the assets that can be used to pay off that debt.

- Cash Equivalency - A quick ratio test can show how much cash your company has coming in to offset its upcoming expenses.

- Collection Periods - A collection test can calculate how long it takes your company's accounts receivables to turn into cash collections.

Inevitably, your company will have to produce an operating statement for lenders, buyers, and CPAs in addition to a balance sheet upon the sale of your company. You may recognize this financial report by its more common name, the Profit and Loss Statement, or the P&L. While the balance sheet details your company's assets and liabilities, the operating statement details your company's income and expenses. Think long-term figures for the balance sheet versus short-term figures for the P&L.

The operating statement can provide the following information about your company:

- Profitability - Derived from the profit margin ratio comparing the net profits (income earned after expenses but before taxes) to your gross sales income (e.g., if you sell $1,000 in a month with a net income of $100, your profitability is 10 percent).

- Return on Investment - Calculated ratio that compares the net profit of your company to your company's net worth (e.g., if your company's net worth is $1,000,000, and it is earning $100,000, your return on investment is 10 percent).

- Inventory Valuation - On a financial statement, the value of your inventory is how much you paid for it. (It can also have a market value, a book value, a liquidation value, and/or a collateral value). To determine if you have too little or too much inventory at any given time, you need to figure up an end-inventory value ratio (e.g., if you paid $100,000 for your current inventory, and your monthly sales are $50,000, you have a 2:1 ratio. In other words, your inventory is two times greater than your sales).

CUSTOMER REPORTS

Inextricably tied to your financial reports are your customer reports. Some companies record customer and sales information directly into their financial software systems, but others use a Point of Sale system that pulls and synchronizes customer and sales information into their financial software systems. No matter how you record customer data, the point here is that you take the time to enter it somewhere.

Essentially, customer reports can highlight the following information:

- Customer Totals – Basic head count of customers, patients, or clients you reach on a daily, monthly, quarterly, or yearly basis. Ideally, these counts will show steadily increasing numbers.

- Customer Retention – A proven number of returning customers, patients, or clients increases your company's customer capital.

- Customer Acquisition Costs (CAC) – Attained by dividing the amount of money you spent on advertising by the number of new customers you gained during that time (e.g., if you spent $5000 on a billboard advertising campaign over four months, and you gained 20 customers, your CAC would equal $250).

- Customer Lifetime Value (CLV) – Identifies the value of long-term customers (e.g., if you determined that you spent an average of $250 to acquire a customer but the customer spends $1000 once or $20 on 30 different times over their lifetime with your company, then your advertising costs are reaping rewards. However, if you spend an average of $250 to acquire one customer, and that customer spends $50 in your store once, then you need to adjust your marketing campaigns or the culture customers experience within your store).

Product and Service Reports

As customers buy your products and use your services, you will be able to generate reports from your software systems about their purchases and about their satisfaction with their purchases.

Specifically, look over the following information:

- Service Tickets – Assessing the number of new, resolved, or open service tickets will give you an indication of how well your service department is responding to customer needs. Your assessment of service tickets can also identify which product or service needs improvement and which service customers request most often.

- Product Loss – Figured by subtracting the number of defective and stolen products from the total products produced during a specific period of time. Your goal is to minimize the loss percentage by decreasing manufacturing and production errors or by increasing your security measures to protect your items on the shelves.

- Product Returns – Identifying which products are returned most often is vital to your research and development department. If customers return one product more than any other, look for manufacturing defects and correct those, or discontinue offering the product.

- Production Efficiency – Measured differently within each industry, you'll take the number of units produced or services offered and divide those by the hours of production to determine how efficiently your company is running.

EMPLOYEE REPORTS

Finally, you can print reports to indicate your employees' production and turnover. Just as you want to see how well your products are doing, you want to see how well your employees are doing to increase your company's efficiency.

- Employee Production – Certain reports can detail individual employee production if you have employees key in numbers or names every time they enter sales in the software system. These reports will indicate sales leaders and followers, allowing you to incentivize ones or retrain others.

- Employee Turnover – Take time to analyze how many employees have come and gone over a certain amount of time to see if you need to revitalize your training systems, your compensation methods, or your company culture.

REAP THE REWARDS

Obviously, you already know what you like about your company and what you don't like about your company. Now, buyers are looking for that, too. They will hire attorneys, CPAs, and CFPs® to pick apart your business to find its strengths and weaknesses, so you might as well use your KPIs to analyze your business before they do.

Long before buyers look into your business, consult your own advisors. Systematically pour over financial reports, customer reports, product reports, and employee reports with them, and analyze the data from buyers' perspectives. Don't stop there, though. Once you identify your company's weaknesses, make the changes necessary to strengthen those deficient areas. Retrain employees on your current systems or create new systems. Inevitably, if you want to increase the intrinsic value of your intangible assets, you must use the data you glean from your systems to reinforce your structural capital.

If you start doing that now, your business's value could shoot through the roof by the time you are ready to sell it, and you might even be able to sell your company earlier than you expected. Either way, you can sit back and reap the rewards of your hard work before you reach sale time.

CHAPTER 18

DEVELOP A MARKETING CAMPAIGN

"Good marketing makes the company look smart.
Great marketing makes the customer feel smart."

Joe Chernov

As you hire talented employees and work to increase their happiness and loyalty, they systematically increase your customers' happiness, diversity, and retention. When customer sales increase, you need to implement strong management systems that can streamline your production and productivity. Then, you need to analyze reports you glean from your financial, Customer Relationship Management, request for proposal, sales, marketing, research and development, talent, legal, and operational management systems to measure your company's growth and its potential for growth. Finally, to maintain and multiply that employee and customer base that you have worked so hard to grow, you will need to implement a systematic, continual marketing campaign.

In other words, as your human and customer capital grow in value, you must demand more of your systems which increases the worth of your structural capital. To maximize the growth rate of your **human**, **customer**, and **structural capital**, you must work on your **social capital**. Social capital is your business's branding and reputation within your marketplace. To maximize the value of your company, you need to develop a consistent and continuous marketing campaign. I have realized over the years that successful business owners need a marketing system just as much as they need a business plan and a solid team.

THE IMPORTANCE OF A MARKETING CAMPAIGN

Over the years, I've worked with hundreds of business owners, managing their wealth and helping them grow the value of their personal and business assets. Inevitably, when we talk about increasing the value of their business capital, we talk about marketing and advertising. In response to my recommendation to begin or continue a marketing campaign, I often hear clients say things like, "Marketing doesn't work," or "Advertising doesn't work." They'll say, "I've spent 'x' amount of dollars before in advertising," and they'll name a specific thing they did and tell me how it wasted their money. I've even heard several say, "I could build a better business just by word of mouth." Perhaps they can. However, I find it interesting that in 2015, Apple—the company that everyone knows, the company that sells phones and tablets, the company that has a cult-like following—spent $1.8 billion on advertising.

Now let me ask you a question. If everyone on earth knows the Apple name, why would Apple spend $1.8 *billion* on advertising? If advertising didn't work, then perhaps one of the most successful companies in our modern history wouldn't have spent $1.8 billion on it. See, Apple knows that there is a return on investment (ROI) when you market and advertise. The ROI may not appear in the dollar amount you expect or within the timeframe you desire, but there is a return on investment.

If large companies of our era are spending billions of dollars on marketing and advertising, what makes business owners say things like, "Marketing doesn't work"? Could their negative experiences be a result of their lack of planning? Could their confusion between the roles marketing and advertising play within their business cause the negativity? Many experiences could taint entrepreneurs' views of this vital source of their businesses' social capital.

THE DIFFERENCE BETWEEN MARKETING AND ADVERTISING

Oftentimes, I find that business owners don't understand the difference between the terms "marketing" and "advertising." In fact, many business owners use the words interchangeably. I'd even say that if you ask 20 business experts to explain the difference between the two words, you'll get 20 different explanations. However, for business owners operating on a shoe-string budget, it's important to understand the difference between marketing and advertising. You must know that the words are not synonymous.

According to the online Business Dictionary, "Marketing is the management process through which goods and services move from concept to customer." It's the "identification, selection, and development of a product," the "determination of its price," the "selection of a distribution channel to reach the customer's place," and the "development and implementation of a promotional strategy."[33] You see, marketing is a company's long-term, systematic plan to convince customers to buy its products or services. Business owners and their team members design and implement marketing campaigns to package and brand their products, to get their products in front of the right people, and to convince customers to purchase their products.

Advertising is slightly different. According to the Business Dictionary, advertising "refers to the process of actually promoting your product or service to the marketplace."[34] Whereas marketing is the strategic **plan** to get products in front of customers, advertising is the actual **promotion** of the products within the marketplace. Your marketing team creates a message, and your advertising team distributes that message.

Neither marketing nor advertising is a new concept to business owners. You've heard these words, and most likely, you've used marketing and advertising in your business. I want to put a spin on the definitions for you, though. *Financially simply* put, marketing is planning *what you want your company to be*, not necessarily what it is today. Advertising is promoting your vision so customers will *want* to buy your products or use your services.

Marketing and advertising work symbiotically to improve your social capital. You should promote your products so that customers in your marketplace recognize your company's name and use your products or services. However,

---

33 BusinessDictionary. (n.d.) Marketing. Retrieved from http://www.businessdictionary.com/definition/marketing.html

34 Glen, Jeffrey. BusinessDictionary. (n.d.) Advertising vs. Marketing. Retrieved from http://www.businessdictionary.com/article/1094/advertising-vs-marketing-d1412/

you want customers to have positive things to say about your company when they see your name or encounter your products. As a business owner, you should want customers to feel good about the products and services they are purchasing from your company. For no matter how often customers see your name or come across your products, they will not buy from you if you have a bad reputation.

DEVELOP A MARKETING CAMPAIGN

If you know that marketing is the preparation, or planning, that needs to be done to get your product in front of your customer, let's talk about how to develop a marketing campaign. I often recommend taking seven steps to accomplish this, but you can take fewer steps or more steps in this process depending on your company's needs.

#1 – Start with your brand.

In marketing, before you do anything else, start with your brand—the color, the typeface, the font, the images, the logo. What do you want people to think about when they see your company's logo? How do you want them to feel? As marketing consultant Kimberly Haydn says, "Branding is about so much more than what people see. It's about how you make people feel." Essentially, you want your audience to connect with your company, and one of the best ways to do that is through branding.

For example, what do you think of when you see a red bullseye? Do you think Target? What comes to your mind when you see an image of a bull with wings? Do you say Red Bull? Do you recognize certain companies when you see a lightning bolt or a swoosh? Sure, you said Gatorade and Nike! Most likely, I didn't have to name the companies attached to the logos I mentioned. The images are interconnected with specific companies, and each image triggers certain thoughts or feelings in your mind. Do you think quality or athleticism? Do you think energy or hydration?

Obviously, companies' logos are important pieces in their branding puzzles. The more customers see a logo, the more likely they are to remember a company and buy its products or services. Customers then begin to associate a company with its brand. If the company that consistently promotes its brand to the public can also consistently provide valuable products and services to consumers, customers will likely return to the company for more products or services. Then, not only do customers associate a company with a brand, they begin to associate positive experiences with the company and its brand. They *feel* good about the company and its products or services, so they *feel* good when they see the company's logo.

#2 – Target your specific audience.

Once you create your logos and qualify your brand, you want to concentrate on your customer. Ultimately, marketing centers around your customer, so you want to target a specific group of people. To target an audience, you must know the audience. Who are they? What do they do for a living? How much money do they make? Where do they shop? Where and what do they like to eat? What do they do for fun? Are they highly educated? Are they hard working? Are they constantly stressed? What do they like? What do they dislike? Do they watch certain television shows or certain types of movies? If you understand your customers' habits, you can advertise directly to them.

In my company, Financially Simple™, my business director and I created an avatar to represent the type of customer we're trying to reach. We named our persona "Frazzled Frank/Frazzled Felicia" because the person we're trying to reach is a professional business owner and entrepreneur who is stretched too thin. Our "Frazzled Frank/Frazzled Felicia" customer has expert knowledge about his/her trade or industry but may not have business or financial know-how. Frazzled Frank and Frazzled Felicia are extremely stressed and need someone to look at their financial lives holistically. Our target customers need an objective third party who is knowledgeable about business and finances to show them how to drive up their businesses' revenue, increase their net worth, or lower their tax obligations.

After describing our ideal customer through this avatar, my business director and I made a list of everything about Frazzled Frank and Frazzled Felicia: their family situations, favorite restaurants, TV shows, hobbies, where they spend time, etc. Thus, when we "talk" to the Frazzled Franks and Frazzled Felicias, we know their problems and pains, their goals, and we talk to them the way they want to hear it… we *know* Frank and Felicia.

#3 – Show up in the right places.

Once you know who you are targeting, make plans to advertise in places your customers will be. If you are marketing to female baby boomers, you're probably not going to put an advertisement on a local rap station because most likely saturations of female baby boomers are not listening to rap music. That's not where you want to advertise.

Instead, you want to develop a marketing campaign that advertises in places female Baby Boomers are most likely to be seen. Get your advertisements to appear on websites through which these women browse. Saturate the radio stations they listen to or the restaurants they frequent. Speak to church groups or ladies' crafting groups. Use the information you uncovered about your avatar to develop marketing campaigns that will advertise directly to your target audience.

#4 – Target the timing of your advertising.

Not only do you want your advertisements to show up in the right places, you want them to show up during appropriate times. Perhaps you're in a business that has seasonal products or demand-for-services like I was in my landscaping years. In that business, we were extremely busy mowing lawns, planting flowers and trees, fertilizing yards, mulching, and creating hardscapes during the late spring, summer, and fall. However, very few customers required our services during the bleak winter and early spring months.

Rather than marketing during those November through March months, we timed our campaigns to begin in late March and continue through October so that we could reach our customers when they would be most receptive to our products and services. Why would I advertise my mowing services in December if no one needed a yard mowed? How could I measure the success of a winter marketing campaign if customers would not use my services until a later date? When I advertised my company's services during our peak seasons, I received more return on my investment than I could have if I advertised in our slow seasons.

#5 – Work on your online presence.

When you are trying to increase the value of your social capital, you want to get social, and many companies do that through online social media because they can measure the results of their campaigns. Obviously, you can advertise through those social media channels, but when you are developing a marketing campaign, you want to concentrate on improving your online rankings.

Although website rankings and online algorithms fascinate me, I understand very little about them, so I rely on my team members who are experts in this field. They know how to get my blog articles, podcasts, and educational YouTube videos to appear when consumers type certain phrases or questions into online search engines. My team tracks my company's standings and followers on my social media channels, and they adjust my tweets or posts as needed to increase our rankings. They also revise the layout of my newsletters to increase consumer traffic to my website.

If you don't know how to optimize your online presence through search engine optimization, hire someone who does. To establish and increase your social presence, you or people on your team must know how to drive customers to your social media and website channels. Not only that, you must know how to present your products and services in such a way that you maintain a good reputation within that online community.

#6 – Create an elevator pitch.

Part of optimizing your social presence online and within your community is honing your company's specific verbiage to your target market. Online, you can test keywords and meta descriptions to improve your content's phraseology. Outside of the online community, you can spend money on word research to identify which words will offend your customers, which words will gain traction, which words will inspire consumer confidence, etc. This type of audience testing reveals how customers will react to certain words you use within your advertisements.

As you create a marketing campaign, you want to research which words will help your target audience connect to your company, your products, and your services. Using the "wrong" words can damage your reputation, just as choosing the "right" words can enhance your reputation and increase traffic to your business.

#7 – Set systems to measure and track the results of your advertising.

Finally, before you implement your marketing plans, make sure you can track your results. Remember, marketing is strategizing how to get your product ready to sell. It is setting systems in place to establish a social presence to reach your ideal customers. Before you can present your message, you must create it and prepare it for measurement. You will set up systems and methods to advertise your products to your target audience. Then, you will ensure those systems and methods offer a way for you to measure the effectiveness of your advertising.

Management consultant, educator, and author, Peter Drucker, famously stated, "If you can't measure it, you can't improve it." Oftentimes, I find that people will throw their marketing dollars into the wind or throw them against a metaphorical wall to "see if they stick." They advertise anywhere and everywhere without a way to measure the effectiveness of their marketing campaigns.

To prevent such flippant waste of your marketing dollars, use online marketing resources like the analytics built in Google AdWords, Constant

Contact, LinkedIn, Facebook, Twitter, or Instagram that track the results of your campaigns. If you do not use online marketing, use your business's Key Performance Indicators that we discussed in Chapter 16 to track the results of your marketing campaign.

CHAPTER 19

MARKET AND ADVERTISE

"Make your marketing so useful people would pay you for it."

Jay Baer

The key to marketing and advertising is consistency, and the key to your business's continual success is marketing and advertising. You must establish a social presence within your target marketplace and create the message you want customers to see. Then, you want to revise your marketing campaign and advertise consistently to "show-off your good side," so to speak. You see, through marketing and advertising, you can improve or change your reputation. You can seek to control how customers perceive your company and its products.

THE BASICS OF MARKETING AND ADVERTISING

Who Should Market and Advertise?

If you are like most business owners, you are always short on time. You may not think you have time to market much less develop a marketing campaign system, especially if you are trying to grow your business to sell it, but that is the furthest thing from the truth. Every person in the organization advertises for your company whether you have a marketing campaign plan in place or not.

Therefore, wouldn't it be best to create a plan so that everyone advertises in a similar manner? If you want to show-off your culture of kindness, make sure all employees are kind. Maybe hire an agency or a team to create a uniform marketing campaign plan that shows the community how kind you are. However you market, remember that all team members are a part of your advertising presentation.

When Should You Market and Advertise?

By default, then, if everyone in your company advertises your values and your message, then you are marketing all the time. However, you should still develop formal marketing strategies from the day you decide to grow your business for its eventual sale, or you should expand upon the one you are already doing. Then, you should continue advertising until you pocket the money from your business's sale. Market and advertise twice as much when times are bad, and market and advertise to shape your persona when times are good.

Where Should You Market and Advertise?

I could easily say that where you advertise depends on your national, state, or local location, and at its simplest, that's true. However, what works for one business may not work for another even within the same industry. Therefore, I try to get my clients to work with an external or internal marketing professional from day one. If you are working toward the sale of your business, find one quickly to redirect your current marketing strategies to the demographics of your market.

If you don't have the money to work with a marketing professional, concentrate on your target audience and where they would be each day. Where will they buy their groceries or eat their food? Where will they shop for home goods or appliances? Target your market, and you will know where to advertise.

How Should You Market and Advertise?

In the previous chapter, I told you how to develop a marketing campaign, so I'll concentrate on how to spend your advertising dollars now. Here are 10 (of hundreds of) ways you can get your message into your marketplace:

1.   Leverage your connections within your community.

2.   Collaborate with other businesses that complement your own.

3.   Purposefully network at local chambers, clubs, bureaus, or events.

4.   Give speeches or seminars to university students or to organizations.

5.   Ask for referrals from satisfied customers.

6.   Interact with your customers on social media.

7.   Write down what you know or do in a blog.

8.   Educate your customers about your products or services through a podcast or YouTube channel.

9.   Offer coupons online or through printed materials.

10. Do a giveaway through a radio broadcast, at your store, or online.

How Much Money Should You Devote to Marketing and Advertising?

Once you have established a marketing campaign, you will need to allocate funds to it. If you have a billion dollars in the bank, and you are producing more and more business, more power to you. Most of us don't have that. Many business owners often feel that marketing is a waste of money because they don't see immediate results. Truth be told, I've even had those thoughts.

Traditionally, though, I tell business owners in certain industries to allocate 5 to 10 percent of their annual revenue toward marketing management, and that is just to *maintain* their current income stream. I find that my clients who want to grow their businesses generally allocate 20 to 30 percent of their annual revenue to marketing campaigns to attract more customers and to maintain their current customer base.

MARKETING IS A BUSINESS INVESTMENT

Throughout my years working with entrepreneur clients, I have learned that marketing and advertising are investments, not expenses. Even though the quantifiable costs will show up on your Profit and Loss Statement as expenses, you are dealing with investments.

Making, implementing, and continuing a marketing campaign is comparable to the laws of sowing and reaping:

1. We reap what we sow.

2. Reaping happens after sowing.

3. We reap more than we sow.

4. We often reap later than we expect after sowing.

If you develop a marketing campaign and advertise to your target market, you are sowing good seeds, if you will. When customers identify you with your brand, and use your products and services, you reap your advertising rewards, and that's why having a marketing system is important.

Simply put, you market to generate sales. You increase your social capital to grow your customer capital. You spend advertising dollars to bring people into your business to buy your product or service. That produces revenue. If you set good profit margins, you will reap the money you have sown times two, three, or four. Theoretically, if you spend $50,000, you could earn $100,000, but you cannot earn it if you do not invest it into marketing and advertising.

However, don't invest the money and then just walk away. Don't quit. Marketing is not a magic pill. Just because you spend $1,000 in January does not mean that you will make $5,000 in February. Marketing is a continual tool that keeps customers coming through your door. It can also bring potential business buyers to your door.

Keeping a clear record of your marketing strategies and their quantifiable results will add validity to your business's systems. Strong systems make you, as an owner, less needed, which makes your company transferable, which makes your company more valuable to a buyer.

OPTIMIZE THE HEALTH OF
YOUR INTANGIBLE ASSETS

"Don't wish it were easier; wish you were better."

Jim Rohn

Your intangible assets consist of the human, customer, structural, and social capital within your business. As you increase the value of each, you raise the value of the others, making your business healthier and more attractive to buyers. Ultimately, they want to know that **your intangible assets work together** to make your business profitable, competitive, scalable, sustainable, transferable, and invulnerable to risk.

CHAPTER 20

MAKE YOUR BUSINESS SCALABLE

"You will either step forward into growth,
or you will step back into safety."

Abraham Maslow

I have always liked the parable in the Bible where Jesus talks about a man who built a house on sand and a man who built a house on rock. In Matthew 7:24-27, Jesus tells his disciples that when the waves came, the floods washed the sand out from under the first man's house, decimating everything he had underneath the water, but when the rain and floods beat upon the rock, the other guy's foundation withstood the waves.

When my wife and I built our dream home in the country, I was particularly fascinated by the laying of our house's foundation. I watched men dig down to reach solid earth before they placed the footer and the piers. At times, the men dug almost 12 feet down before finding solid ground. After laying the base, the workers poured concrete and laid rebar, and did everything that had to be done to give my house a firm foundation.

Just like a house, your business must have a sound foundation. *If your business plan and your value growth plan are the blueprints for your business, then your capital assets—tangible and intangible—are your business's foundation.* The more improvements you make to that foundation, the more sound it becomes.

Once you lay and strengthen your business's foundation, you can build up the frame of your company by making it scalable, profitable, sustainable, transferable, and competitive. However, after you finish framing your business, you must protect its structural components by putting up drywall, sheetrock, brick, rock, stucco, and/or vinyl siding. In other words, you must make your business invulnerable to risk.

Since we have already discussed increasing the value of your assets, especially your intangible assets, let's dive into building the framework of your business— its scalability, profitability, sustainability, transferability, and competition.

WHAT IS SCALABILITY?

Throughout this book, I have essentially defined a successful business as one that will sell for the desired profit and terms at the desired time. I realize that you cannot reach that successful business completion without some sweat equity, but unfortunately working hard is not the only key to success. No, probably the most important thing to building a business successful enough, or valuable enough, to sell for profit is increasing your business's scalability. Your hard work must go into making your business scalable in nature.

Then, what does scalable mean? Simply put, **scalability is the capacity to expand your business according to market demand**. If you have a highlighter or pen handy, circle or highlight the word, "capacity." Capacity is "the facility or power to produce, perform, or deploy."[35] Notice that by definition, "capacity" is the *facility* or *power* to produce something; it is not the production of it. In other words, it's throttled energy or power, not unbridled energy or power.

I like to think about scalability, or capacity, in terms of a sports car. Most people buy sports cars because they are built to go fast. They have the ability to travel at speeds over 200 mph, and they have the power to go from 0 to 60 miles per hour in just a few seconds. That's their appeal. Yet, just because the car *can* go 200 mph doesn't mean a driver *should* drive 200 mph all the time. That's ridiculous. Anyone driving a sports car must follow posted speed limits or face fines. You wouldn't see a sports car flying past you at 200 mph in a school zone! Sure, *it can*, but at that moment, it doesn't need to go that fast.

A business's scalability works the same way. Your business needs to have a strong enough infrastructure to "go fast." You need to have the facilities, sys-

35 Merriam-Webster (September 2, 2018). Capacity. Retrieved from https://www.merriam-webster.com/dictionary/capacity

tems, and manpower available to increase production when needed. However, just because you *can* produce 200 widgets per minute doesn't mean you *should* always produce 200 widgets per minute. You don't want to produce more than you can sell at any given time, but you want to be able to produce an enormous amount quickly if and when the market demands it.

INCREASE OUTPUT AND MAINTAIN COSTS

Sometimes, increasing production in your business means turning your proven product and proven business model into a franchise and opening store fronts all over the nation or the world.[36] However, that is not necessarily your goal. *The business value growth I am talking about with scalability revolves around the capacity to increase output (production, sales, revenue) while decreasing or maintaining costs (labor, production, supplies).*[37]

If you operate your business out of your garage or from the trunk of your car, chances are you can't increase your production until you open a storefront, move your operations into a warehouse, or hire employees. Yet, can you do that and keep your profit margins the same as they were when you were a one-man or one-woman show? Similarly, if you handmake every product in your inventory, chances are you can't increase manufacturing without hiring others to help you make the product or without purchasing a machine that will make the product for you.

As you are working to increase the value of your intangible capital—your human, customer, structural, and social capital—then you are building the foundation upon which you can scale your production. The stronger your capital is, the healthier your business is, or the more scalable it is. Ultimately,

36 Zwilling, Martin. Forbes. (September 6, 2013). 10 Tips for Building the Most Scalable Startup. Retrieved from https://www.forbes.com/sites/martinzwilling/2013/09/06/10-tips-for-building-the-most-scalable-startup/#1e962e4c5f28
37 Housh, Will. Entrepreneur. (March 12, 2015). Choosing a Business Model That Will Grow Your Company. Retrieved from https://www.entrepreneur.com/article/243237

increasing output while maintaining costs leads to greater profit margins, or profitability.

We'll talk about the value of your business's profitability in the next chapter, but before we get to that, let's figure out how to make your business scalable so that you can make it profitable.

1. **Hire all-star employees.**

   Depend on others to help you. More than likely, you can't scale your business without bringing in qualified team members. You'll need help, and the more talented your team members are, the more ability they'll have to perform tasks well and efficiently. Furthermore, the more self-motivated they are, the more likely they'll be to work independently of your help and watchfulness. Their ability and self-sufficiency will help you increase your business's productivity and your own productivity.

   Maybe your team members aren't extremely talented when you hire them but they're willing and able to work hard. Invest the time into training them to produce, sell, or serve the way you want them to produce, sell, and serve, but as you hire and train talented team members, don't forget to pay them what they're worth.

   A well-compensated, all-star team member will likely produce 10 times the product, sales, or revenue than less qualified or less motivated team members will produce. Thus, while you may pay your all-star team members more than you would pay an average employee, your all-star team members should be producing enough or more to offset their higher rate of pay.

2. **Institute versatile management systems.**

   Next, you'll want to begin, upgrade, utilize, or invest in management and technological systems that will streamline your processes and procedures. Use a Point of Sale software system to track your Requests for Proposals, your bids, your Purchase Orders, your Accounts Receivable, your Accounts Payable, and your inventory. You can't scale production if you're keeping track of orders and inventory on scrap sheets of paper that end up all over your office. If possible, connect and synchronize your Point of Sale software program with your financial services software program so you don't waste time duplicating data.

Go back to Chapter 15 and review other types of management systems that can help you streamline production. Look into Customer Relationship Management software systems and into research and development processes. Develop an efficient quality control process. Create team member workflows for each of your business departments.

Then, look into purchasing other technologies that can help you save time and money. Review new products and equipment in your market. Purchase technological items that will help your employees work smarter, not harder. Can you manufacture your products twice as fast if you purchase a piece of machinery or make an assembly line? Can you see twice as many patients within an eight-hour time period if you invest in a state-of-the-art x-ray machine?

When deciding whether to purchase new equipment, machines, or technologies, make sure you're spending your money wisely. Don't buy new "toys" just to brag about having them. Do your homework and research. Ensure that the systems you purchase offer a quick return on investment, an increase in production, *and* a decrease or maintenance of your current expenses.

3. **Create scalable product solutions.**

Once you have talented team members and versatile management systems in place, examine your products and services. Business owners' time, money, and expertise are in constant demand, and implementing systems will require much time, money, and expertise, but coming up with ways to make your products or services more lucrative should not require as many of your valuable resources. To maximize your business's profitability and revenue, you can identify areas within your product or service lines that can be increased or reduced quickly and easily by simply answering the following questions and others like it:

- What product/service do you offer that has the highest profit margin?

- Which product/service has the potential to reach double-digit growth rates?

- What product/service can your team easily explain to the marketplace?

- Which product/service can secure outside leverage?

- Do you have a product/service that is easy to market?

- Can you automate one of your products/services?

- Can a product/service be franchised, licensed, or duplicated?

Your answers to the questions will show you how to take a product or service you offer and begin to scale it up. Yet, you want to scale up production without increasing labor or supply costs. Maybe you need to outsource your manufacturing to another country to do that. Perhaps you need to invest in machinery that will automate your services or automatically make your products. In other words, what you learn about your products will help you increase revenue and decrease costs to increase the value within your business.

4. **Market and advertise.**

When your team and your systems are ready and able to increase production of your products or services, it's time for you to implement your marketing system and advertise said products and services. That's the last piece of your scalable puzzle. Unless you have more customers coming through your doors or demanding more products and services, you have no reason to increase production or scale your business.

SCALABILITY LEADS TO PROFITABILITY

Remember, you are working on building value within your company to make it enticing or sellable to buyers. If you want to sell your business for the most money possible, then one of the things you must do is make your business scalable. You can do that by investing time, energy, and/or money in your team members, your systems, your products, and your advertising.

If you don't have the cash capital to invest in new technologies, make sure your business's infrastructure is set up so seamlessly that it can sustain rapid growth with a new influx of capital when an investor buys your business. People buy businesses that make money, and businesses with the capacity to grow typically bring larger price tags because by scaling your business, you make it more profitable.

CHAPTER 21

INCREASE YOUR PROFITABILITY

"Business must be run at a profit, else it will die. But when anyone tries to run a business solely for profit, then also the business must die, for it no longer has a reason for existence."

Henry Ford

REVENUE IS NOT PROFIT

A t the beginning of the book in the section, "Why This Book Matters," I shared the Exit Planning Institute's statistic that 80 percent of business owners' net worth is tied up in their business. Thus, it only seems right to me that if my business comprises most of my net worth, that business better be pretty doggone healthy. I mean, if it is the horse I am going to ride into retirement, then it better be fed, groomed, watered, and brushed. This business of mine better look like a show horse, right?

For a business to be healthy, it must be profitable. In other words, your business must bring in more income than you spend on business expenses. How, then, do you make it profitable? Well, ***profit is not the same thing as revenue, nor does high revenue equal profitability***. While you must earn money to become profitable, if you spend too much of that income, you will never actually "make" money.

Take my experience as an example.

When I started my landscaping business at 15 years old, I thought I was making money hand over fist. I thought I was rolling in high cotton. If I worked a job where plants cost me $1,000, then I would charge my customer $1,200. That was a 20 percent "profit" margin! I was on top of the world, thinking the sun came out just to hear me crow, so when I didn't have enough money to pay myself at the end of the month, I couldn't figure out where all my money was going.

Although I thought my 20 percent margin was all profit, I didn't take into account my costs for fuel, supplies, new tools, taxes, or the like. Sure, I brought in a lot of money, but when I wrote off my expenses, I didn't actually *make* any money. If I had wanted to sell my business at that point in my career, no one would have been interested in it because it was not profitable. However, once I learned what I was doing wrong, I fixed the problem, made my business profitable, and sold my business for a profit years later.

THE 5 X 5 X 5 GROWTH TECHNIQUE

But how? How did I do it? For that matter, how do you do it? Well, among an arsenal of techniques I use as a financial planner, I find that the 5 x 5 x 5 Growth Technique seems to help business owners increase their profitability quickly because it gives them quantifiable goals that show them when they have become successful.

Originally created by Craig West, a Certified Exit Planning Advisor from Australia and teacher at the Certified Exit Planning Institute, the 5 x 5 x 5 Growth Technique challenges business owners to:

1. Increase sales by 5 percent.

2. Increase gross margins by 5 percent.

3. Decrease selling, general, and administrative expenses (**SG&A expenses**) by 5 percent.

Increase Sales by 5 Percent

The first "5" percent deals with your gross sales. You want to increase your total sales by 5 percent, and you can do that a number of different ways—coupons, offers, incentives, marketing, advertising, upselling, employee training, etc.

Basically, you increase sales by increasing the value of your four Cs! Because each business and industry is unique, I can't tell you which method will bring the most customers through your doors, nor can I cover all of the sales-boosting methods available to you, but I can challenge you to use some kind of method to increase your sales by 5 percent.

Increase Gross Margins by 5 Percent

The next "5" percent challenges you to increase your gross margin, or your net income divided by your gross income that you find in your financial reports. In reality, that's not a lot. If you are already at a margin of 40 percent, I'm not telling you to reach a margin of 45 percent. No, what I am saying is that you will multiply your 40 by 5 percent, which equals 42 percent, so you are just increasing your margin from 40 to 42 percent. You can accomplish that. Perhaps you need to outsource production of your product to Mexico or China. Maybe you need to hire or fire key employees. Whatever it is you need to do to increase your margin, you can increase it by 5 percent.

Decrease SG&A by 5 Percent

When you get to the last "5" percent of this growth technique, you want to decrease your selling, general, and administrative expenses. Essentially, you want to spend less on expenses you can control. Maybe you ask an insurance agent to review your policies to see if you are paying the lowest premiums possible for the best insurance available. Perhaps you start buying generic office supplies or shopping at wholesale outlets for general store supplies. No matter how you decrease expenses, you want to assess your unique business operations to see where you can cut corners without cutting quality or service.

TOPLINE TO BOTTOMLINE

Whether you use the 5 x 5 x 5 Growth Technique or another technique to increase your business's profitability, you want to earn above-average revenue, have below-average expenses, and make above-average profits. That is the bottom line. If you increase sales through customer capital but do not decrease expenditures, then what will that profit you?

To maximize the effectiveness of your techniques, be sure to talk to a CERTIFIED FINANCIAL PLANNER™. That advisor can help you pull more money into your business while helping you spend less and develop a profitable margin so that you can decrease the value gap between your business and others in your industry. Only by decreasing that value gap will you be able to vie for business sellability within your marketplace. You will never be in the top 20 percent of businesses that sell if you cannot show proven profitability over a significant period of time.

CHAPTER 22

RECOGNIZE THE DIFFERENCE COMPETITIVE ADVANTAGE MAKES

"You should learn from your competitor, but never copy. Copy and you die."

Jack Ma

WHAT IS COMPETITIVE ADVANTAGE?

If a medical practice, a restaurant, and a retail store sit on every street in your city, what makes patients or customers choose your establishment over another? Why would someone travel further, pay more, or overlook small personal inconveniences to use your services or buy your products? What makes you special? What sets you apart from your competition?

Simply stated, competitive advantage is what makes your business better than its competition in the minds of your customers. Competitive advantage can even be one of the factors that bring customers into your store, which is part of increasing your business's profitability.

To me, Henry Ford is one of the most intriguing entrepreneurs of our time because of how he leveraged his company's competitive advantage. Since the "Ford" name remains notable and branded some 120 years after he began his business, most people believe he invented the automobile. Yet, Henry Ford didn't invent the first car; he created something completely different, and THAT is what led to his success.

Ford figured out how to physically arrange machines and people in such a way to produce more products faster than the competition. Thus, he invented the assembly line, and mass production became his competitive advantage, leading to his fame and fortune.

WHAT DOES COMPETITIVE ADVANTAGE LOOK LIKE?

I recently read an article in which Kimberly Amadeo, economic analyst and business strategist, states, "To be successful [in business], you need to be able to articulate the benefit you provide to your target market that's better than the competition." Exactly. You must have something or do something unique to draw customers to you right now and to entice buyers in the end. Not only that, your social capital must be strong enough to articulate the benefit of your competitive advantage to existing and potential customers so that you can increase the value of your customer capital.

Are you starting to see how this all ties together? If you have a product or perform a service that no one else in the industry can provide or do, your business will be more valuable than your competitors', which can drive up the value of the multiplying factor in your business value equation. For example, if you and Company B each average $100,000 adjusted EBITDA, but you have a patented product that Company B does not have, a business buyer might determine business value as follows:

Company B's Value:

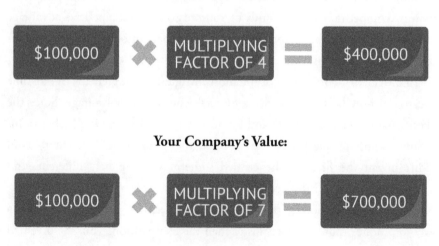

Your Company's Value:

Note the difference in company worth. EBITDA does not differ; what makes the difference in value is your competitive advantage.

THE DIFFERENCE A COMPETITIVE ADVANTAGE MAKES

Recently, I was talking with a client of mine about what makes customers spend their dollars one place versus another. We spoke specifically about Chick-fil-A®, a fast food franchise in the Southeast that makes chicken entrees. While I think their chicken sandwich is the best I've ever put in my mouth, neither the sandwich nor the waffle fries set the company apart from industry competition.

What, then, sets the company apart? Could it be that employees say, "It's my pleasure" when they serve customers instead of asking if "you want fries with that?" Could it be their highly efficient drive-thru line, where servers take orders WHILE cars are in line rather than at the end like others? Well, both matter. Chick-fil-A® secures its competitive advantage in the fast food industry with its exceptional customer service model.

Likewise, companies like BMW and Tesla® secure their competitive advantages in the automotive industry with unique and luxurious design features. Apple and Samsung™ make their companies more valuable than others through technological innovation and marketing strategies. Pepsi® and Coca-Cola rely on brand recognition to gain and keep customers.

CHAPTER 23

IDENTIFY YOUR COMPETITIVE ADVANTAGE

*"It's not about being better. It's about being different. You need to give
people a reason to choose your business."*

Tom Abbott

THE MOST COMMON TYPES OF COMPETITIVE ADVANTAGE

As different as the industries themselves, companies can make a name
for themselves from among dozens of different competitive advantages.
Marketing specialist, Anna Mar, identifies six sources of competitive advantage she believes are most noteworthy in the business world.[38] Assuming your
business practices one of the following, I will delve into each of the six Mar
identifies.

People

This advantage is not about the number of owners, managers, or employees
your company has, nor is it about your company's gender, age, or ethnic ratios.
No, this competitive advantage is about the willingness of your team members
to go above and beyond their basic duties.

I often think of Disneyland® and Walt Disney World® here, and one story I heard comes to mind. While on their first visit to Disneyland® a young
family stopped in front of the iconic Partners statue depicting Walt Disney
and Mickey Mouse holding hands. Seeing two of the park's "Cast Members"

---

38 Mar, Anna. 6 Sources of Competitive Advantage. (April 2013). Retrieved from https://
business.simplicable.com/business/new/6-sources-of-competitive-advantage

(employees) cleaning the area, the father asked them how to get to another attraction. Rather than handing them a map or pointing them to a park guide, these two street sweepers slung their brooms over their shoulders, had the family line up in a single-file line and marched the whole crew across the park to reach their destination. On the way, these men hopped, skipped, and laughed with the kids. They even took a few photos of the family together for the family's memory books. The Cast Members' actions made such an impact on this family that the mother wrote to Disneyland® executives and said, "Your people are amazing."

This competitive advantage is also about identifying and utilizing an individual team member's strengths. Savvy employers will place employees in roles and positions that will highlight strengths and manage employee time and energy most efficiently.

Think about it this way. Professional or collegiate football teams have 50 to 100 players on their rosters. Each player has unique skill sets and abilities, and each is uniquely qualified for his role. For the organization to win games, it must ensure that the team functions as one, living, breathing unit instead of as 100 individuals. If a member of the team gets hurt or isn't pulling his weight that day, another person can slide in for the common good of the team.

You see, one of the strongest competitive advantages a business can have is a remarkable team. If you invest in your team and include them in your short-term and long-term goals, they will buy into your objectives. They will want everyone they know to experience your product, and they will make sure customers have positive experiences when they purchase the product. If you get buy-in from your team, you have a rare, valuable commodity.

Organizational Culture

Companies that create value through culture do so through many months and sometimes years of intentional training. Businesses that clearly define, enforce, and reinforce their expectations, their philosophies, their values, and their rules for interactions between owners and employees, employees and colleagues, and employees and customers usually create a strong, united corporate culture. How a company conducts business and treats its employees and customers can greatly affect the business's most basic productivity, its general performance, and its employee performance.[39]

If business owners make their employees feel valued and essential, the employees will most likely have more positive attitudes. Customers then pick up on that positive attitude, or culture, and may feel better about spending their dollars at your establishment rather than at a competitor's.

Processes and Practices

While many companies can make and sell related products or provide comparable services, companies can set themselves above their competition by creating unique manufacturing methods or service processes.

A restaurant in my hometown of Brunswick, Georgia offers an example of this competitive advantage. While the owners of Willie's Wee-Nee Wagon combine a passion for good food with a love for people, neither their cuisine nor their customer service separately sets the company apart from others. No, one menu item—the restaurant's pork chop sandwich—puts this restaurant on the map.

Chefs smother this sandwich with a combination of "commonplace" ingredients that give the pork chop sandwich a unique look and taste. It is so deliciously unique that the company owners issue a direct challenge to their competitors on the side of the building. They declare, "If you can find a better pork chop sandwich, we'll give you $2,000 cash." They put their money where their mouth is, so to speak, and they have such a competitive advantage that no one else in that area even attempts to make or sell a pork chop sandwich to compete.

Products and Intellectual Property

Many companies utilize the fourth competitive advantage, and you may have established your own business around it. Your products are new and innovative

39 Business Dictionary. Organizational Culture. (n.d.). Retrieved from http://www. businessdictionary.com/definition/organizational-culture.html

in design or technology. Their uniqueness means that you must protect your rights to that intellectual property through patents, copyrights, or trademarks.

Without legal protection, competitors can replicate your product and take away your competitive edge. Take the iPhone. Apple created a piece of technology that is very difficult to replicate. Samsung™ tried, but Apple sued them and won its case, keeping its exclusivity to the product and design.

Service-based industries can still have this competitive advantage, but logistics get a little trickier. For instance, before the publication of this book, my company, Financially Simple™, did not have a consumable product other than my podcast. I know that people can listen to my podcast and record something similar, but they cannot replicate my intellectual capital. I have 40 years of unique experiences, and other people cannot use the examples I give in my podcast because they did not live them.

Intellectual capital is inherently unique to its owner, but others can use your outlines or systems if you do not protect your copyrights. If you can highlight your product's unique design or your unique service process, you can drive up the value of your product or property. If your product's value increases, so does the valuation of your business.

Capital and Natural Resources

Maybe you do not have unique people, processes, products, or services but you do have money and lots of it. Go back to Apple. Today, that company has more money than many countries in the world and its cash capital is almost impossible for others to replicate.

Perhaps you have social capital rather than cash assets, and 200,000 followers and subscribers may hang on your every word on Twitter, YouTube, or in your email lists. Your competitors cannot purchase or achieve that type of capital overnight. Thus, it makes your business valuable to potential buyers.

Just like a client of mine in West Virginia, you may own land that naturally produces oil, natural gas, ore, or coal. The resources themselves are insanely valuable, but if you can use the products your land produces free of charge to power your company's equipment, you can significantly lower your cost of goods or services. No other business can duplicate that, which drives up the value of your business.

Technological Advancements

The last most common type of competitive advantage combines intellectual property and capital. Technology evolved into a powerful business asset during the Industrial Revolution at the turn of the Twentieth Century.

Go back to Henry Ford. Many businesses, including his, were building cars because the technology was easy to duplicate. However, Ford set himself apart in the industry by creating the technology of the assembly line. His technological advancement decreased his product turnaround time and lowered his company costs, making him a powerful and rich man.

If your business can create a form of technology or technological system that none of your competitors can easily replicate, then you have a valuable competitive asset.

FIND YOUR NICHE

While most of my business owner clients find their competitive advantage within the list of six I mentioned above, technologist John Spacey lists and defines 40 types of competitive advantages in the business world that include niches like scalability, variety, know-how, reputation, and location[40]. You can see examples of companies that use Spacey's types of competitive advantage daily:

Orvis® and Darn Tough Socks stake their reputations on the long-lasting quality of their products.

Walmart® and Kentucky Fried Chicken™ have a scalable worldwide presence.

Walgreens and CVS Pharmacy® compete for prime real estate locations.

40 Spacey, John. 40 Examples of Competitive Advantage. (November 2015). Retrieved from https://simplicable.com/new/competitive-advantage-examples

Honestly, your competitive advantage may define your vision and determine what type of business structure you choose as you begin your company. It may be the reason you opened your business in the first place. Whether it inspired your company's beginnings or whether it provides a structural layer of your business, competitive advantage can exponentially increase your company's value, which increases its multiplying factor.

If you are building a business to sell it in 10 years, you want to make it as valuable as possible to potential buyers. One of the easiest and quickest ways to increase your company's worth is to create a competitive advantage within your industry. Find your niche. The harder it is for your customers to leave or the harder it is for your competitors to duplicate your systems, the more valuable your business is to buyers.

CHAPTER 24

EXPAND YOUR BUSINESS'S SUSTAINABILITY

As discussed in Chapters 8-10, you must determine your business's current value to see if a value gap exists between what you could make versus what you stand to make at this moment if you sold your company. If you decide to invest the time and effort into accelerating your business's value to make a profitable return on your investment when you sell, you must also calculate how much of a cash reserve your business needs to withstand tough times that will inevitably come before you list your business for sale. No matter how strong your intangible capital is, how deep your plan to grow value within your business is, how wide your margins are, or how scalable your service is, if your business does not have enough in its cash reserve to survive financial storms, selling your business will be a nonissue.

FAST CASH AND BIG SPENDING

During the years 2004 through 2007, I observed an interesting economic phenomenon. Seemingly, everyone and his brother was jumping into the home construction business. I remember people leaving their long-time jobs, going to banks, borrowing half a million dollars, and building massive houses. Many aggressive individuals managed to make some fast cash during that time.

As I watched the market boom, I noticed something else. Sure, these entrepreneurs were making significant cash revenue, but they were also dramatically increasing their lifestyle expenditures. They were living high on the hog, if you will. Well, all is well and good until it isn't. Beginning in 2007, an economic downturn thundered through the nation. Because many of the "quick buck builders" spent their thousands as quickly as they made them, they didn't have cash reserves to weather the storm, and ultimately, many declared bankruptcy.

SQUIRREL IT AWAY

A key, if not *the* key, to business survival, is to start with enough money to get through the tough times. To withstand the storms that will eventually come in your business, you must build a company that has sustainability. In other words, you must have enough cash reserved to reach consistent profitability.

Those who know me know that I spend a lot of time in the woods, and one of my favorite things to do is to sit in the stillness of God's beautiful creation, watching His creatures. Most fascinating to me is their innate ability to survive, and their sustainability seems to depend on their preparedness. As summertime turns into fall, I watch squirrels run around the woods in search of acorns and nuts, stashing them away as quickly as they find them. Inevitably, wintertime robs the woods of its foliage and its resources, but the squirrels have the food they need to help them survive the barren season.

Since you are preparing your business to sell it within the next 10 years, you have already weathered the startup phase of your business, so your sustainability at this point depends on your ability to squirrel away enough money during seasons of prosperity to survive the coming barren seasons. Without substantial resources to sustain profitability, your business will most likely dissolve or be liquidated to your creditors in bankruptcy court.

HOW MUCH DO YOU NEED?

In 2011, Chicago business owner, Jay Goltz, published an article in *The New York Times* titled, "The Top 10 Reasons Small Businesses Fail." Ultimately, Goltz's reasons boil down to business owners' lack of planning, lack of scalability, lack of knowledge, lack of compromise, lack of management, lack of profitability, lack of quality, lack of margin, and lack of cash capital.[41] From my own observations as a CERTIFIED FINANCIAL PLANNER™, I find that

---

41 Goltz, Jay. The Top 10 Reasons Small Businesses Fail. (January 2011). Retrieved from
    https://boss.blogs.nytimes.com/2011/01/05/top-10-reasons-small-businesses-fail/

many businesses simply do not have enough "cash capital," or cash reserves, to weather the storms and the barren seasons that inevitably come.

Then, how much cash do you need? How much cash reserve will be enough to sustain you through the tough times? Well, in most circumstances, businesses can predict capital needed with a pro forma[42] (projected) financial statement, and the methodology within that hypothetical calculation applies to almost all types of businesses. Therefore, let's walk through this process:

1. *Decide how many more years you want to work before you sell your business.* Since I have used 10 years as my standard in this book, I will use that number.

2. *Calculate anticipated recurring monthly, quarterly, and yearly expenses you will incur during that timeframe.* Let's assume you will spend $500,000 each year, totaling $5,000,000 over a 10-year period.

3. ***Conservatively*** *estimate the gross income you expect to receive during that timeframe.* Remember, we are looking at a doomsday scenario. Hypothetically, then, let's say you expect to earn $450,000 (***at the very least***) each year, totaling $4,500,000.

4. *Subtract your projected income from your predicted expenses to calculate the shortfall,* $5,000,000 minus $4,500,000 equals $500,000.

Your projected $500,000 shortfall is the bare-bones amount of cash reserve your business will need for sustainability, for survival amidst the forthcoming storms.

Do not stop there, though. Notice that I said "bare-bones amount." I like to add another 25 or 30 percent buffer into my projected business cash needs. Therefore, if my calculations tell me I need a $500,000 cash reserve, I might want to begin with $625,000 to safeguard myself against unforeseen circumstances. To receive a complementary downloadable pro forma along with more details on using this valuable tool please visit https://financiallysimple.com/pro-forma-financial-statements/

---

42 For a sample pro forma, visit https://financiallysimple.com/pro-forma-financial-statements/

FUNDING

By this point, you may be saying, "Justin, do you honestly think I'm going to be able to 'squirrel away' that ungodly amount of money when my business is barely getting by day-to-day as it is?"

This *can* work. You can find funding for cash capital and cash reserve, but the funding available will most likely depend on how realistic your pro forma is. With a strong, projected financial statement, you can apply for a bank loan or line of credit on your own, or you can contact the Small Business Association (the SBA) for help finding a lending institution that specializes in small business loans. Do you have any ties to outside investors or loan sharks? Perhaps you can tap into a rich family member's pocket.

If you decide to apply for loans or to ask others for financial assistance, your pro forma will be vital to secure funding. Jonathan Mills Patrick, one of the top SBA investment lenders in the state of Tennessee, explains that banks and investors look at your pro forma to determine whether you have enough cash coming into your business to repay a loan. *After* making sure you have the ability to repay, Patrick explains that banks will look at your collateral and your cash on hand (your liquidity) to determine whether or not they can offer you funding.[43]

What happens, though, if you do not have that cash on hand? Most business owners look for loans because they are short on cash. Well, folks, it's time to squeeze your quarters so tight the eagles scream. Save, save, and save. Then, save some more. Cut expenses. Get stingy. Sell personal assets or assets the business does not use anymore. Find a way to set aside cash reserves.

STASH THE CASH

Remember, though, that the purpose of borrowing this money, reserving access to this money, or making this money is *to save it*, not to spend it. Unlike requesting a loan from a lender because you are in desperate business straights,

---

43 Funding Options – Investor vs Bank Loan https://financiallysimple.com/investor-vs-bank-loan-which-is-the-best-source-of-startup-capital/

you are securing funding to use *if* and *when* your business enters dry seasons; you are not procuring a loan to pay down current business debt or to buy new equipment. This will be your cash reserve, not your payday.

Do you remember me mentioning that cash flow is king when it comes to your business's sellability? Your business's sustainability is where that cash flow and cash reserve come into play, so keep it. Squirrel it away. Protect it. Invest it. For most business owners, I recommend that you keep a minimum amount of operating cash in your business and put the rest into accounts or investments outside the company that you cannot get too easily but that you can convert to cash quickly.

I recommend that you separate the majority of your business's emergency fund from your cash accounts for a few reasons:

1. You earn little to no interest in a business checking or savings account.

2. If you leave a significant amount of cash in your business accounts month after month or year after year, potential buyers may assume that amount of cash is needed to operate the company.

3. You will be tempted to reinvest the majority of the money back into your company.

You do not want to sabotage your business's sellability unintentionally by leaving too much money in your business bank accounts. Therefore, when you get the business loan or as you diligently save the money for your business's cash reserves each month, set aside 10 percent, 15 percent, or 20 percent of the gross to create a business emergency fund. Then, do whatever it takes to get more customers. When times are good, pour extra income back into marketing and advertising so more people know you are around. Furthermore, take care of the customers who come through your door so that when customers must be stingier with their money during the rough times, they will come back to you instead of your competitors.

Storms will come while you are preparing your business to sell it. Maybe they come through literal floods, earthquakes, or tornadoes. Perhaps they come when loved ones fall ill or family members begin feuding. What if the stock market crashes or the political climate changes? No matter how the storms come, you know they are coming.

Therefore, analyze your margins to ensure your business's profitability. Secure your competitive advantage within your marketplace, and scale your production to keep up with demand. Yet, do not stop there. Reserve cash as a safeguard against the storms. Even if you build your business on the proverbial rock, without additional cash reserves, cushions, or protections around your entity, you could be swept away by the waves or receive a pittance in return for your investment.

CHAPTER 25

ELEVATE YOUR PERSONAL SUSTAINABILITY

"Focus on making yourself better, not on thinking that you are better."

Unknown

REACHING THE FINISH LINE

To decompress from long hours at work, I enjoy exercising, and I like to mix up the type of exercising I do. Consequently, I choose to train for triathlons because I can swim, bike, and (somewhat) run. I absolutely love swimming, and I don't mind bike riding, but I hate running. It makes my knees hurt, but by doing all three, I feel like I get the most comprehensive workout possible.

I signed up to participate in a half Ironman triathlon in 2017. I was training hard and preparing for the race but then some health issues arose. Some 30 days before the race, my doctor told me that I had to take a break from exercising to get my body healed. Nonetheless, I had committed to doing the race so I showed up, but I crashed on mile six of the run. Actually, I smelled pizza, so I took a detour to eat some pizza and then I just quit.

To have finished that race, I needed to eat better, train harder, and exercise longer than I did. Thirty days of idleness did not sustain me through the 1.2-mile swim, the 56-mile bike ride, *and* the 13.1-mile run. I didn't even take the time to mentally prepare for the race through meditation and proper sleep. Ultimately, I hadn't stored up enough energy within my mind or body, and I used up my reserves before I finished the race.

PREPARE YOURSELF AS YOU PREPARE YOUR BUSINESS

Preparing for a triathlon is not much different than preparing a business for sale. Building value within your business to make it sellable or attractive on the market is hard work, folks, and going through the sales process does not get any easier. Both take a lot of time and energy. Strength and resolve become more important than speed. If you have not adequately prepared yourself for this grueling journey, your physical body or mental stability could give out before your company does. If you want your business to survive trials and tribulations, don't you want to make it to the finish line with your business? Your business's survival, its sustainability, is one thing; your personal sustainability is another.

Business owners are notorious for burning the candle at both ends. Typically, you spend 60, 70, and 80 hours a week working on your business. Since eating, sleeping, resting, and exercising do not appear to contribute to your business's immediate competitive advantage, profitability, scalability, or sustainability, you do not make them priorities in your life.

However, ignoring your personal needs will eventually lead to a crash within your business. Your physical body cannot sustain lack of sleep, poor diet, and constant energy consumption. When your physical body starts to break down, your mind will begin to lose its clarity and sustainability as well. With both physical and mental fatigue affecting your abilities, your business's capability will struggle as well. How can you make logical decisions with no sleep or direct your team from a hospital bed?

MAKE A PERSONAL SUSTAINABILITY PLAN

Yes, spending time working on your business is important. However, spending time taking care of your physical health and mental well-being is equally important. As you plan to exit your business and build value within it, make a personal sustainability plan. Include time to:

Sleep

If you have to, write down the actual time you should be in bed at night to get the sleep your doctor recommends you personally need. More than that, don't bring work to bed. Leave it, and turn your phone on vibrate. You can accomplish more tomorrow after a good night's sleep than you will tonight with no sleep.

Eat

Plan client meetings at restaurants during lunch, or have a team member bring in food at a certain time each day. If you meet with sales representatives, have them provide team lunches while they teach continuing education courses or do product presentations. Do NOT leave meals to chance. Know what you will eat and where you will eat each day so that you don't forget to eat or forget to eat well.

Exercise

Even if a typical gym membership is not feasible for you, movement can be. You don't have to lift weights or run five miles a day; you just have to move. Run up and down the stairs in your building once or twice every hour. Get your blood flowing by doing some jumping jacks at your desk. Walk to the mailbox. No matter what you do, just find times and places in your normal day to add movement. Exercise can help you sleep better and metabolize your food better, too.

Meditate

Practice yoga, pray, have quiet time, read, spend an hour with a therapist, or do whatever else you can do to give your mind a break from the stress of daily business. Your mind cannot focus without rest. Personally, I like to sit at the piano when I'm stressed and play for a few hours. It has become my go-to method for de-stressing.

Relax

To me, relaxing is not the same as sleeping or meditating; it is time spent doing something you love to do, something that makes you happy. Whether it's spending time on a hobby, spending a day on the lake, or going to a movie, do it. Schedule a back massage or a lunch with friends. Your happiness should contribute to your business's success, not be a victim of it.

I realize that the self-care plan seems incredibly simple. You may think it's a bit ridiculous even, but take it from someone who has been in business for 26 years. You will take time for yourself one way or another. Either you will make a plan for self-care, or your body will demand care. Whether your body shuts down, the good Lord stops you, or your family demands time of you, something will happen, and you will make time one way or another. Why not do it on your own accord?

Why not take a little bit of time over the next few months or year and invest in yourself? It really is that simple. If you are not sustainable personally, your business will never be sustainable. Your team will fall apart. Even your family could fall apart. I have seen it all throughout my years working with clients. I have seen business owners file for bankruptcy and divorce. They have been hospitalized or stricken with preventable diseases. To prepare your business for its sale in 10 years or less, you must take care of it and create value in it. To make it to that business sale alive and in good health, you must be physically and emotionally prepared.

CHAPTER 26

TRANSFER OPERATIONAL DUTIES TO YOUR EMPLOYEES

*"No man will make a great leader who wants to do it all himself
or get all the credit for doing it."*

Andrew Carnegie

For your business to reach its growth potential and attract buyers, you must take the focus off yourself in your business. You would not be where you are in business today if it were not for the people around you, so take a step back to understand that you are building a business that can operate without your daily presence, your artistic ability, your knowledge, or your abilities. You want to focus on your team members' talents and drive them toward success as a *coach* instead of the star player.

But why? Why do you want your company to operate without you?

TRANSFERABILITY IS KEY

The businesses that can operate without the owner present tend to bring the highest market value at sale time. Buyers do not want a business's success to depend on one person. The strengths of your management team, or the group of people who run the company when you are not there, and the abilities of your entire team make your company more attractive to investors. The deeper your bench goes, or the stronger your human capital is, the higher your sales price goes.

Think about this. If you go to sell your business, and every business decision and process depends on you, the owner-entrepreneur, what will the buyer do when you're not there? Who will know how to operate the company, implement the business plan, and ensure the management systems run seamlessly? No one. No one will know what to do, which makes your business *non-transferable*.

More than likely, the investor-buyer will not want to get into the thick of business operations like you did, but with a management team in place who can operate the business with or without you, your business is going to be much more attractive to a buyer who's looking to make an investment in a company that can double or triple its value *without* their involvement.

Your company cannot reach its full growth potential unless you relinquish control of your business. You must let go of the reins. Without an effective team present, your business will plateau and become stagnant because everything depends on one person's physical and emotional capabilities. Without talent around you, you can only drive your business so far.

CHANGE YOUR WAY OF THINKING

How, then, do you change your way of thinking? How do you make your company autonomous and easy to transfer from your ownership to new ownership?

Let Go of "This is Me" Thinking

You must turn the conversation of your business from "I" to "We." Stop thinking, "I'm the business owner who started this." Instead, start thinking, "We have an outstanding business." Turn from "my" to "our." Go from "This is my" to "This is our."

Be the Coach, Not the Star

You didn't become successful on your own; somewhere along the way, someone invested in your life. Maybe it was a family member, a friend, a pastor, a teacher, or a coach, or maybe you read an inspirational book or blog post that changed your life's direction. Inevitably, somebody in your life has dedicated or sacrificed time, money, and energy to help you. It is time for you to do that now. If you are going to build a scalable, transferable business, you must be the coach and cheer your team on to the victory.

Build the Right Team

As the coach of a team that will ultimately run the day-to-day parts of your business, you need to hire the right people. Do not look for "cheap talent." If you hire less-than-the-best people, you will get less-than-the-best results. Instead, hire the best people you can afford because great people tend to yield great results.

Get Help

Sure, you can run the company by yourself. For the most part, you know what to do but you still need somebody in your corner. You will need encouragement and financial advice, and you will need an objective person to point out your failures and motivate you to successful value growth within your business. Whether it's one of your advisory professionals, a family member, a friend, or a board of advisors, you will need help to stick to your plans.

Remember Your Family

If you are like most entrepreneurs, then you spend much of your time building your business to the detriment of your family, but you must make time spent away from your family the exception, not the habit. To build a scalable business, you will have to walk away from your business once you have all of your systems in place. If you have become a stranger to your family and friends, what will you do? Who will be left with you when you reach success and have time to enjoy life?

CHAPTER 27

MANAGE RISK

"Risk comes from not knowing what you're doing."
Warren Buffett

N ow that you know what areas of your business exponentially increase its value, you must protect that value. You are not spending months, or years, or a decade working on increasing the worth of your company only to let it dissolve or implode before you get to the sale of your business. If you cannot protect your human, customer, structural, and social capital that make you profitable, competitive, scalable, sustainable, and transferable, you will likely lose any chance of selling your business or selling it for profit. Therefore, before I dive into the actual process you walk through when you sell your business, let's take a moment to assess and manage risks that could affect your business's value.

AN EXPENSIVE EDUCATION

A wise person once told me, "Somebody else's experience is a far better teacher than our own." I wish I had listened to that advice. If I had understood the vital role of a business risk assessment in the purchase or sale of a business, I might have avoided making the single biggest mistake of my business career.

Many years ago, I had the opportunity to purchase a business. It appeared, by all standards, to be a very good opportunity, so like any prudent business person, I began conducting due diligence. From interviewing employees and customers to looking at financial statements, I went through this company with a fine-tooth comb, and I didn't even stop there. I sought counsel from attorneys, CPAs, and other professional advisors.

While doing a risk assessment of the business, I can remember asking myself, "Do I really need to buy this business? Should I really add this much stress to my life?" Like an angel sitting on my shoulder, my conscience warned me over and over not to purchase the company. To my detriment, I ignored the red flags I saw on the list of cons, and I began focusing on the pros of buying the business.

Well, I purchased the company and what had seemed like minor discrepancies in the business assessment at the beginning ended up becoming MAJOR problems by the end. Ultimately, I wish I had listened to my gut and the risks that appeared in the assessment. If I had, I wouldn't have bought the company. The excitement about the potential of making more money, though, got the better of me, and it cost me years of my business life.

Not long after making the decision to purchase, I found myself entrenched in a legal battle that cost me over $200,000 in legal fees and seven years of my life. I earned a doctorate degree in risk management from the School of Hard Knocks, and that is a tuition I won't soon forget. Holy Batman! What an expensive education!

TYPES OF BUSINESS RISK

No matter what type of business you own, your business will face risks. Success in business is never guaranteed, and you are bound to encounter hardships and uncertainties. Whether the struggles come systematically to every business owner in your marketplace or unsystematically to you alone, they come. Increasing your business's sustainability and your personal sustainability will help you weather the storms, but you have the option to do more than survive the ramifications of risks. You can predict and prepare for some business uncertainties:

- Systematic Risk

  Often referred to as "common risks," systematic risks are the market uncertainties all businesses and business owners face in a certain geographic location, regardless of their industry.[44] In relation to businesses, these are the risks and changes that occur beyond your control like environmental disasters or weather-related catastrophes. Systematic risks could be changes in national, state, or regional political parties. They could come in the form of new labor, privacy, or sanitation laws. Rises and falls in economic markets, securities, and interest rates also fall into this unpredictable risk category.

- Unsystematic Risk

  Equally uncertain yet *sometimes* more predictable are your business's unsystematic, or "specific" risks.[45] These are the types of uncertainties your business faces by being part of a specific industry or by being part of your life. In other words, these risks are unique to you or your type of business.

  Unsystematic risks could come in the form of an employee divulging trade secrets or going to work for a marketplace competitor. Perhaps you run across high employee turnover or degree-specific job positions that are hard to fill. You could face claims against your copyrights or patents. Machinery you use could break down, or your equipment may become "ancient" quickly in today's technologically advanced world.

  On a more personal level, unsystematic risks could include your spouse's loss of employment, your child's health crisis, or your teenager's automobile accident. Maybe you face medical issues that leave you partially disabled or unable to work within your company. Perhaps

---

44 BBA Lectures. (n.d.) Difference Between Systematic and Unsystematic Risk. Retrieved from https://www.bbalectures.com/difference-between-systematic-and-unsystematic-risk/
45 BBA Lectures. (n.d.) Difference Between Systematic and Unsystematic Risk. Retrieved from https://www.bbalectures.com/difference-between-systematic-and-unsystematic-risk/

Depression affects your mental wherewithal to work consistently or to work well during certain periods of time.

Before you can manage risk, you must identify predictable and known risks. You must know which laws govern your industry currently and comply with those laws. You know, the biggest mistake I ever made was not looking at ALL the potential risks involved with buying a company, and the risk I ignored had to do with legal risks. I missed it clear as could be. My advisors didn't tell me about it, and I was too blinded by ambition to see it. Most of us see the upside of owning a business but rarely do we see the full potential of the devastation of the downside. You must be aware of ALL the various types of potentials risks, and you must follow the laws that govern the risks. As I heard my attorney say over and over, "Ignorance is not an excuse not to obey the law." You've definitely got your hands full.

COMPLETE A BUSINESS RISK ASSESSMENT

What, then, are you to do with these risks? Whenever you decide to sell your business, you should sit down and do a risk assessment on your company. If you do not sell your business immediately, you should sit down every year and do a new risk assessment because risks change. Your state may issue new employment laws, or a competitor may open his doors down the road from you. Interest rates could change, tax laws could be issued, or political party majorities could change.

With so many different types of risk, you need to begin assessing which ones make a difference in your business. For the clients I work with, I recommend completing the following six steps to evaluate risks:

1.   **Consult Outside Counsel** - Start with a good insurance agent who works to protect you from everyday risks. Then, talk to your attorney, your CPA, and your CERTIFIED FINANCIAL PLANNER™ to identify and forecast potential risks.

2. **Seek Internal Advice** - Rally your family and your advisory team, and perform a *S. W. O. T.* analysis. Identify **S**trengths, look for **W**eaknesses, find **O**pportunities, and guard against **T**hreats.

3. **Weigh Probability** - Rank your identified risks in order of how likely they are to occur. Start with the most likely, and finish with the least likely.

4. **Predict Harm** - If your greatest risk is not harmful to your company, don't devote countless time and energy to it. Instead, manage the risks most likely to cause you harm.

5. **Address the Risk** - Do NOT ignore ANY of the risks. Use your rankings and your predictions to decide which ones need immediate attention, but don't turn a blind eye to any risks.

6. **Monitor for Changes** - Shoot for yearly risk reviews to keep up with legal, economic, or political changes.

A risk assessment is not rocket science. Any potential buyer will look closely at your risk management process to see if you understand the risks in your business and to see if you are prepared to handle the effects of those risks. Buyers will want to look at your risk management track record to see if you are prepared for and have battled the risks successfully. They want to see that you have lowered your potential risk factors.

Put yourself in a buyer's perspective. The last thing a buyer wants to do is come in and purchase a business with holes in its risk management shield. If buyers realize you haven't paid your workers' compensation insurance or your employee payroll taxes, they might walk away from your company. You have not spent all your time and energy growing your business in hopes of selling it for millions only to leave holes in its foundation. If you ignore parts of your business's risk assessment, you will most likely lose a buyer's interest in the future, so NOW is the time to take a risk assessment of your business. Prepare yourself, and prepare your company.

SELL YOUR BUSINESS FOR PROFIT

*"The first part of success is 'Get-to-it-iveness;'
the second part of success is 'Stick-to-it-iveness.'"*

Orison Marden

GET YOURSELF READY FOR THE SALE

*"Often when you think you're at the end of something,
you're at the beginning of something else."*

Fred Rogers

After you have worked to increase the value of your business by strengthening and protecting its assets, it is time to reevaluate your business's worth. Bring back that Certified Valuation Analyst®, and have him recalculate your business's value. If you have implemented your growth plan successfully, your business should be worth much more than it was 10 years ago (or any other significant time period you spent working to accelerate the value of your company). Assuming you succeeded, it's time to sell!

CHAPTER 28

ASSESS YOUR NEEDS

"Rational optimism does not start with rose-colored glasses.
It starts with a realistic assessment of the present.
It starts with realism, both the good and the bad.

Shawn Achor

After you have worked to increase the value of your business by strengthening and protecting its assets, it is time to reevaluate your business's worth to receive an actual offer. Not only is it time to call in your Certified Valuation Advisor to quantify your company's new worth, it is time to determine the minimum sales price you need before a buyer quantifies it for you. Sure, you have known what price you want for your company for 10 years or so, but have you taken the time to make sure your ideal price will sustain you and your family in the next stage of life?

ON YOUR MARK, (DON'T) GET SET

In 2017, I participated in a half IRONMAN triathlon. For those of you unfamiliar with a triathlon, athletes swim, bike, and run long distances back-to-back. For this race, I was training to swim 1.2 miles, cycle 56 miles, and run 13.1 miles. Because I try to do one or two of these races a year, I can tell you that they can be absolutely exhausting.

I signed up for the race in January of that year and began training immediately. However, about 60 days before the race, I was at my doctor's office and he told me not to exercise for the following four to six weeks! No way, Doc!

How in the world was I supposed to do that? I had financially committed to this race, and I had been training for it for months. My doctor was persistent though and told me that jeopardizing my health was not worth the risk of exercising for that time, so I didn't.

I did not train. I did not ride a bike or swim or run. It was "fun." For those of you who have done any type of sports, you know that a couple of weeks prior to the race, your conditioning should be at its peak. You must be exercising, but I could not. However, I decided to run the race anyway because I had committed to it, and many friends, clients, business team members, and family members were going to be there watching or participating themselves, and guess what? Those participating had been exercising but not yours truly.

GO!

When race day arrived, I showed up committed but not necessarily ready. Swimming is my thing, so I wasn't worried about the swim at the beginning. The bicycling? I am pretty confident about the bike section, but man do I hate running! Lord, help me if I can get through the run. It's like eating an elephant one bite at a time.

The signal was given, and off I went! The first leg, I hit the water and knocked that part out. I ran to the transition area to put on my biking shoes and helmet, and off I pedaled. I was doing well, but around mile 46 into the 56-mile bike ride, I hit the wall. Holy Batman! Parts of my body were hurting, not just aching, because I had not been able to condition myself. I even experienced the worst cramp in my hamstring I had ever felt before, but I pushed through it and transitioned to the run.

13.1 miles. Yep. Here we go.

BUT WAIT! THERE'S PIZZA

Did I tell you this foot race was a looped one that was set up in two, six-mile loops? Well, as I turned into mile six, I was feeling pretty bad. Just about that time, my business colleague who had been behind me passed me and yelled, "Look dude! They've got pizza at the finish line!"

Now, if you've listened to any of my podcasts or watched any of my YouTube videos, you know that I LOVE pizza. If I could eat pizza every day of the week, I would be in heaven. (Honestly, I have a mission in life to be sponsored by a US-based pizza franchise like Papa John's, Pizza Hut, Pizza Inn, or Jet's Pizza.) All someone has to do is say the word "pizza" and my mind loses motivation to do everything else. At this point in my race, too, I was completely exhausted so what did I do? I exited "stage left!" I walked, because there wasn't any more running at this point, straight through the finish line at mile six. Everyone was cheering me on, and I got a big medal, but all I cared about was eating pizza.

After I finally ate my pizza, I went to the race officials and fessed up. "Guys, I'm sorry. I didn't do the two full loops on the run. I smelled pizza." Thankfully, everyone laughed but truth be told, I'm not sure that I could have finished that race.

DO A PERSONAL ASSESSMENT

What do leg cramps and pizza have to do with selling your business? Just like preparing for a triathlon, you cannot go into the sale of your business unprepared. Heaven forbid you find yourself in the middle of a business sale and realize you are not in shape for that "event." Having the mental fortitude, the financial fortitude, and the emotional fortitude to get through this sales process will be vital to finishing the sale, so before you jump into the sales commitments and purchase agreements or the sales team and the expenses, you need to stop and do a personal assessment to determine the minimum business sales price you need *before* the buyer puts his own price tag on it.

When you reach the end of your 10-year growth plan, do you know what you are going to do next? If you are 50 years old, can you afford to retire now? Kudos to you if you can! Do you know where you will live or what kind of vehicle you will drive? Would you like to cook your meals at home or eat every meal in fine restaurants? How will you obtain and pay for health insurance and medical expenses that arise? Would you like to sell this business and start another one? Your answers to these questions will tell you what dollar amount you need from the sale of your business to live the lifestyle you want to live afterwards.

Your answers to those questions also determine the type of quantifiable personal assessments you should do at this point in the business sales process, so I ask you to stop, pause, and look at your person. Then, ask yourself the following questions before you begin your business sale:

1.   **How will your cash flow be affected?**

One of the most popular and problematic things I see in selling a business is that business owners do not understand the cost of capital. For example, a friend of mine was preparing to sell a business that produced about $12 million a year in revenue, and he didn't have many Cost of Goods Sold, or COGS, inside the business. After analysis, we determined that he was running a 15 to 17 percent income rate on this business. In other words, he was taking home about $1.8 million (15 percent of $12 million) per year. However, if he sold the company for a minimum sales price of $18 million, the proceeds would only generate about $900,000 per year in take-home income ($18,000,000 x a hypothetical 5 percent = $900,000). Thus, you must look at your pre-sale and post-sale cash flow scenarios. Will your cash flow after the sale be enough for you to live the life you want to live, whatever kind of life that is?

2.   **Will a sale affect your personal tax planning?**

If you receive a "nice check" that supersedes the minimum sales price you expect from the sale of your business, what will your personal tax repercussions be going forward? Do you need to stop now and make some adjustment to the way you have positioned your assets to minimize future tax liabilities?

You see, right now, if you need additional capital, you just work harder or generate more sales, but what happens when you go from the entrepreneur phase to a retirement phase? How will you generate additional cash flow to offset whatever tax demands the government requires of you?

3.   **Are your risks managed?**

While your business required multiple types of insurance and legal documents, what types of insurance and liability coverage will you need now? Do you really need life insurance anymore? Will you need long-term care insurance, disability insurance, or health insurance upon retirement? You should assess your current insurances and legal requirements as a business owner and determine which ones you will need after the business sale.

4.   **How will you manage your investments?**

Whenever you sell your business, you are most likely dealing with taxable accounts. In my years as a CFP®, or CERTIFIED FINANCIAL PLANNER™, I have found that most entrepreneurs are strategists, and instead of worrying with stocks and bonds, the owners I have worked with prefer to position their money where it will grow in the most efficient way possible. Therefore, you need to look at your investment management process. Hire a CERTIFIED FINANCIAL PLANNER™, and develop a plan to minimize your taxes and taxable income assuming you sell your company.

DETERMINE THE MINIMUM BUSINESS SALES PRICE YOU NEED

After you reevaluate your business's worth, you need to requantify your personal assets. Will you have enough money on which to live after you sell your company?

Look back at Chapter 3 of this book where you planned your retirement, or your life after the sale of your business. Have you saved enough in your illiquid savings accounts (like retirement accounts) and in your liquid savings accounts to retire when you sell your business? Can you claim social security benefits now, or do you have enough money to live without them? Have you met your predicted personal budget, and can you continue to meet it after the sale? Do you need to work longer within your company before you sell it, or do you need to find a different full-time or part-time job after the sale?

After running personal and business valuation assessments, you may find a different type of value gap exists now. Sure, your 10-year focus on value acceleration may have eliminated the value gap between your business's worth and the worth of your leading industry peers, but is there a difference between the appraised value of your company and the minimum sales price you need to meet your life goals? That type of value gap can occur at many different business and personal levels, so it's time to find out if it exists. Now is the time to look for any remaining gaps—before you put your company on the market. Right now, before buyers offer to buy your company, is the time to determine your minimum business sales price.

I tell you this information because the last thing you want is to embark on this metaphorical IRONMAN race of selling your business unprepared. You do not want to find yourself in the final stages of your run and realize that the buyer's offer will not meet your needs.

Unlike my IRONMAN race where I could just walk out and grab a piece of pizza, you cannot walk out of a business sale without losing hundreds of thousands or millions of dollars that are on the table. If you go into this business sales process without knowing what your company is worth after you have increased its value or without knowing the minimum sales price you need to cover your personal expenses, you may have to walk away. Walking away could damage your overall personal and business worth significantly. Additionally, if you walk away in the middle of a sale, you could harm your potential buyer base. If the sale does not go through, your next potential buyers may end up giving you a low-ball offer.

CHAPTER 29

PLAN YOUR EXIT

"Every exit is an entrance somewhere else."

Unknown

Many business owners believe that they will build such an exceptional business that one day a buyer will swoop in and make them instant millionaires, but that is a fairy tale, friends. Business doesn't work that way. If you have spent years growing your business to sell it as a valuable commodity but you have not prepared yourself to leave the company, then you will never reach the sale. I believe that when you want to sell your business, you should begin at the end. Therefore, at the beginning of this book I recommended that you make a decision to sell your business long before you plan to sell so that you can create a viable business plan and growth plan. By following and updating those plans along the way, you can reach a profitable end of your business.

Just as I recommended those two plans, I am going to recommend a third. To reap the capital rewards from the seeds of value you have sown over the past 10 years, I believe you should create an **owner's exit plan**. Once you have received a new valuation for your company and determined your minimum sales price, now is the time to reassemble your advisory team to create this last business plan—the owner's exit plan.

DESTINATION SETBACKS

Growing up, my brother and I spent a lot of time outdoors. Like many country boys, some of our fondest memories come from four-wheeling around the countryside. Because it was mostly swampland, we spent much our time getting muddy. One day, we had gotten particularly nasty, dirty, and stinky so before we headed home, we decided to take a swim in the lake to wash it off. We jumped on one four-wheeler, double-heading with my brother driving and me directly behind him holding on to his waist, and we set out on a back trail toward the lake.

While we were cruising through the deep woods, I heard my brother yell, "Duck!" Well, he ducked, but I wasn't fast enough. I was still looking for the duck flying through the air when my entire body wrapped around a South Georgia pine limb. Smack! I rolled off the four-wheeler and found myself lying on the ground, looking up at that wretched tree limb.

Well, my brother was laughing his head off, and I was lying there in pain. Luckily, I was not permanently or unalterably injured, but I definitely experienced a setback toward my goal of swimming and playing in that cleansing lake water. We did end up making it to the pond that day, but it was so late by the time we got there that we didn't get the long, relaxing dip we were hoping for. We only had time for a quick rinse.

KEEP GOING TO YOUR END DESTINATION

Like I had plans to journey to the lake, you have a plan in place to get to the sale of your business. That is your "lake" destination. You and your team have jumped on the proverbial four-wheeler, and you have driven that way. At some point, though, a South Georgia pine limb is going to get in between your current plans and your ultimate goal. That tree limb could be legal issues, employee troubles, family drama, or health concerns. You name it; you will experience some type of setback, and you are going to get knocked off the four-wheeler.

However, you must get back up. You have to get back to the four-wheeler even if you are limping. You may have to brush off the jeers from family members or friends. You may even get muddier, but you have to suck up your pride and get to that swimming hole no matter what. The muddier you get, the more you will appreciate the dip in that promised cool fountain.

Since you made the decision to sell your company some 10 years back or so, you know what your swimming hole looks like by now, and you know where it is. Up until this point, you've been swimming in the pool of business growth, but it is time to prepare yourself for the dive into the waters of the business buyout.

AN EXIT IS INEVITABLE

Although I cannot predict the exact timing of your business's sale, I can predict one thing for certain. You will leave your business. That is an inevitable fact of life. However, how you leave it is still uncertain. Will you die before you retire or sell? Will you be forced to dissolve the business or liquidate your assets, or will you be able to sell your business to a family member, friend, or investor?

You must know by now that you will not own this business forever. At some time in your life, you will exit your business by fate, by force, or by free will. Therefore, it makes sense for you to plan your own exit just as you planned your business's future and your business's growth. No matter how strong your original business plan is or how successful your growth plan has been, you will never be able to walk away from this amazing company you have birthed and parented if you are not mentally prepared to leave it. If you have not come to terms with letting someone else buy your business, you might even pass up millions of dollars!

As a Certified Exit Planning Advisor®, one of the most amazing things I see during the business sale is owners walking away from a buyer's dream offer. If you have spent all these years building the value in your business to sell it for profit, why would you back out? What makes some business owners take the money and run, so to speak, and what causes others to turn down millions of dollars to keep working their fingers to the bone?

Ultimately, I find that some business owners are scared of living their lives without working in their business. All they have known is business, and they don't know what else to do. They have not mentally prepared for retirement, and that makes their future beyond business ownership extremely precarious.

Never planning the emotional toll you will endure when you sell the company into which you have poured blood, sweat, and tears could cost you valuable opportunities. If you plan to sell your business and you plan its growth but you do not plan your exit from it, your emotions may prevent you from walking away with a check in hand. Not planning the retirement and life you have dreamed of before the business sale happens could make you reticent to sell.

MAKE AN EXIT PLAN

You can do things now, though, to prepare for the wave of emotions that will come with your business sale. Draw up an exit plan that includes the following details:

1. **Decide what you will do after you sell** - Make personal plans to travel, golf, take care of grandkids, spend time on a hobby, or begin another business before you leave this one.

2. **Gather your team** - Let your professional consultants, board members, employees, family members, and friends know what your personal exit goals are so they can hold you accountable for reaching them.

3. **Establish a timeline** - Decide how quickly you want to walk away from your business after its sale. Decide now whether you intend to stay to help the new owner and current employees or walk away as soon as you sign on the dotted line.

4. **Make a step-by-step financial agenda** - Make detailed plans now for what you will do with the proceeds from your business sale. If you and your advisory team lay out a detailed financial agenda, you will have the money you need to enjoy your life of leisure or your next big venture.

5. **Hold your team accountable** - Just as your team is holding you accountable, hold them to the fire also. Do not let anything slip through the cracks that could leave you or your company vulnerable at its time of sale.

You may be a person who constantly develops plans, but you cannot start or implement them. Maybe you are the person who starts 20 things but cannot finish one, or you are the person who has your hand in 1,001 different things. Whether acting, finishing, or prioritizing is your weakness, I have the same word of caution for you. It is way too risky to jump right into business OR the business's sale without having a plan. Many times, it is impossible.

Creating an owner's exit plan can provide you with timelines, agendas, financial estimates, and accountability. Walking through the "what-if" scenarios can help you prepare for the next step in life. Additionally, if you make preparations to leave your business and do something else, you will begin stepping back from day-to-day operations. That leads to a business's sustainability and scalability which increases its transferability. Don't you like how that all works out?

Folks, the best designed plans do not do you any good unless you act, so get back on the four-wheeler and go toward the swimming hole. It is time to move toward your business's sale and to prepare yourself mentally for it. NOW is the time to act. Right now is when you need to prepare your owner's exit plan.

CHAPTER 30

CHOOSE A SALES FACILITATOR

*"Sales are contingent upon the attitude of the salesman
— not the attitude of the prospect."*

W. Clement Stone

Once you and your professional advisory team determine that you are, indeed, professionally and personally ready to sell your business, you will need to bring more professionals into the sales "game." At this key moment in your business's life, it is time to bring in your special teams, and to do that, you must first choose a business broker, an M&A Advisor, or an investment banker to facilitate your business sale negotiations. You will need a team member who can initiate and mediate your interactions with potential buyers.

In fairness, the broker, the advisor, and the banker provide similar services in a business sale. However, each has a different skill set that provides different advantages and disadvantages for buyers and sellers. Therefore, let's identify the players, look at their skill sets, and decide which player you need to assist with the sale of your company.

POTENTIAL SALES FACILITATOR #1 - THE BUSINESS BROKER

Let's start with the business brokers. Also known as business transfer agents, or intermediaries, brokers act as mediators between buyers and sellers.

- Who Do They Serve?

Typically, business brokers serve smaller, local, or regional "mom-and-pop" companies that gross less than $7.5 million in yearly sales. According to the US Small Business Association, around 30.2 million companies fall into this small business category.[46] Those companies usually sell for less than $5 million and sell to individual buyers. For the most part, they also have less than one million dollars in **EBITDA**, or **E**arnings **B**efore **I**nterest, **T**ax, **D**epreciation, and **A**mortization.

- How Do They Get Paid?

Business brokers do not tend to charge sellers an upfront fee for services. If they must clean up a huge mess to get the seller positioned to sell, however, they may charge an initial set-up fee but most of the time they do not. Instead, they often charge a commission that funds and pays them at the time the business sells.

- What Do They Expect from the Sellers?

Additionally, business brokers require the seller to compile a multitude of materials to prepare for the sale. Those could include marketing materials used, past and present financial reports, or financial forecasts. In medical fields, brokers might ask for total patient counts and demographics. Sellers may even have to list what types of procedures, services, or products they offer and how many they provide or sell on an average day. Although sellers will have to provide quite a bit of documentation to brokers, they do not usually have to go to an accountant for help or additional compilations.

- What Benefits Do They Provide?

Like REALTORs®, business brokers walk sellers, and sometimes buyers, through the sales process. Facilitating brokers can list the business

---

46 U.S. Small Business Administration Office of Advocacy. (2018). 2018 Small Business Profile. Retrieved from https://www.sba.gov/sites/default/files/advocacy/2018-Small-Business-Profiles-US.pdf.

for sale, develop marketing strategies to attract buyers, arrange business walkthroughs, meet with buyers' agents, answer questions, and help negotiate sales terms and conditions if issues arise. Essentially, business brokers put lipstick on the business to make it look pretty to attract a buyer.

Brokers also act as cushions, or emotional barriers if you will, between the buyer and the seller. The brokers' objectivity and creativity can repair hurt pride and can dampen fiery tempers if the sales process does not go according to plan.

POTENTIAL SALES FACILITATOR #2 - THE MERGERS & ACQUISITIONS ADVISOR

The next professional able to stand in as your special teams' player is the Mergers & Acquisitions (M&A) Advisor. These agents bridge the gap between the business brokers' small businesses and the investment bankers' large companies.

- Who Do They Serve?

    M&A Advisors will typically work with national or international companies that gross between $7.5 million and $100 million in yearly revenue. According to the Strategic Exits Corp, these mid-sized companies usually sell for $12 to $15 million and have a $30 million EBITDA range.[47]

- How Do They Get Paid?

    Like business brokers, M&A Advisors will work on commission dependent upon the size of the sale and upon the closing of the sale, but M&A Advisors could charge additional fees. Charges can include,

---

47 Strategic Exits Corp's Exit Strategies Workshop: http://www.exits.com/blog/exit-strategies-workshop-helsinki/

but are not limited to, initial set-up fees, tax structuring fees, legal structuring fees, or legal service fees.

- What Do They Expect from the Sellers?

Since this business sale potentially merges companies across state or continental lines, M&A Advisors will require more documentation from the sellers than a business broker does. The larger the business, the more complex the sales process gets. To calculate an accurate value of the company's worth and a credible sale's price, M&A Advisors need documents, reports, and pro formas from all locations and from all CPAs working with the locations.

- What Benefits Do They Provide?

M&A Advisors can match buyers and sellers like business brokers. Unlike brokers, though, M&A Advisors can help arrange financing, provide outsourcing, structure the transaction, and provide legal or tax advice if they have lawyers and accountants on their own team.

POTENTIAL SALES FACILITATOR #3 - THE INVESTMENT BANKER

Seemingly out of left field, investment bankers come into play, and they provide services that business brokers and M&A Advisors typically do not.

- Who Do They Serve?

Usually, investment bankers work within the large international business space left by the brokers and advisors. Companies in this realm tend to sell for $100 million or more and operate in a similar EBITDA range.

- How Do They Get Paid?

Like the others, investment bankers can make a percentage-based commission upon the sale of the business. However, they can also charge for services by the hour. If the business sale or acquisition includes stock shares, they could get paid a percentage of stocks shares or in-stock options.

- What Do They Expect of the Sellers?

Because of the complexity of these types of international transactions, investment bankers require a broad litany of complex financial, logistical, and historical business documentation. Sellers will need an army of lawyers and CPAs to digest data points and explain terms and conditions within the deal.

- What Benefits Do They Provide?

Unlike most brokers and advisors, investment bankers are formally licensed as broker/dealers within the Securities & Exchange Commission. This means that they can move privately held businesses into publicly traded companies. They can also provide a broader line of financial services because of the multiple team members, attorneys, and CPAs their firms have on hand.

CHOOSING THE BUSINESS SALES FACILITATOR YOU NEED

As discussed, three different players can facilitate your business sales process, but how do you know which one to choose?

- Apparent from the discussion above, size matters. Your company's revenue and valuation will likely determine which professional you choose. Business brokers usually take care of small business sales under $7.5 million. M&A Advisors tend to handle mid-size mergers between $7.5 and $100 million, and investment bankers guide the reins of the large company sales over $100 million, so the sales price helps you determine who you need on your special team.

- Equally important to you, the buyer matters. If you are selling to an individual, mom-and-pop buyer, you will probably choose a business broker. However, if you are dealing with private monies like syndicates, hedge funds, or international corporate buyouts, you are probably going to use an M&A Advisor or an investment banker.

- Finally, help matters. Brokers are good at handling relatively simple sales transactions. If you don't need much help, and your deal is fairly simple, a broker may be all you need. On the other hand, if you are dealing with a bit more complexity, multistate laws, or multi-country laws, you could choose an M&A Advisor or an investment banker. For consideration, if you need to get your company to auction, you will most likely require the services an M&A Advisor can provide.

Having special facilitators on your team is vital as you prepare to sell your business. They will walk you through the entire process and make your business look and smell good to potential buyers. As my dad would say, "They'll put lipstick on that pig."

As you walk into this business sales process, your core advisory team members (the CPA, the CFP®, and the attorney) can help you identify which special teams' player you need to use. While each facilitator can help connect buyers and sellers, each one has a unique skill set, and each plays in a different marketplace.

CHAPTER 31

DECIDE HOW YOU WILL SELL YOUR BUSINESS

"Opportunities don't happen. You create them."

Chris Grosser

A fter hiring a sales facilitator, you and your broker, M&A Advisor, or investment banker will need to determine *how* you want to sell your business. Can you make the most money by selling your company through an auction or a through a private sale?

SELLING YOUR BUSINESS THROUGH AN AUCTION

Depending on your personal preferences, your personality, and your professional team's advice, you may choose to sell your company through a controlled auction.

If you have ever been to an auction or seen one on TV, you've likely seen a fast-speaking auctioneer rattling off requests for bids. At some auctions, silent and calm audience members will raise hands, fingers, or number cards to indicate their intent to purchase the item up for sale. Event planners at these types of auctions will use increasingly valuable product offerings to drive up audience excitement, participation, and valuations.

In contrast, other auction venues encourage loud and sometimes raucous bidding environments. They want audience members to yell out bids and talk over other participants. In this case, event representatives hope that excessive noise and hyped-up emotions will increase excitement and participation levels.

Essentially, they use the high intensity of controlled chaos to drive up bid values.

Similar to the two types of auctions I mentioned above, you have two basic ways to solicit buyer bids. On one hand, you can quietly and privately accept bids, quotes, or letters of intent from a small group of buyers. On the other hand, you can auction off your business to a controlled group of pre-qualified buyers. Obviously, your goal is to get top dollar for your valuable company with terms favorable to you and to the buyer. However, your personal preferences can make a difference in whether you sell your company through a private auction or a listed sale.

TOP REASONS WHY YOU WOULD USE AN AUCTION TO SELL YOUR BUSINESS

As a business owner, you might choose to list your business for sale through an auction for one or many of the following reasons:

- Competition can drive up the bidding/sales price.

- You don't want a price cap to limit buyer offers.

- Your product or service is in high demand and will attract multiple bids.

- A strategic buyer is interested in your company and needs a gentle prodding to make an offer.

- Buyers are already making offers before you have listed your business for sale.

- Your Dream Team is worth their weight in gold.

- You are selling within the middle market, the $7.5 million to $1 billion arena.

Your M&A Advisor or investment banker may be the best sales facilitator to use if you fall into this middle market company size and decide to auction your business, but regardless of who you use to help sell your business, use a professional's guidance and help.

THE BUSINESS AUCTION PROCESS

If you decide to sell your business through an auction, this type of auction will not look like the ones you see on TV. You won't gather buyers into one room and let a fast-speaking auctioneer demand bids from audience members. Buyers won't raise hands or numbers, neither will they yell out bids. No, that is not the type of auction you will hold.

What does the business auction look like, then? How does it work, and what will you and your business sales facilitator do during this process?

In its most basic form, you and your exit team members will follow these basic steps:

1. **Identify potential buyers** - Privately or publicly publicize your intent to sell your company to attract identified and unexpected potential buyers. Once you know who is interested and how many people are interested in purchasing your company, your next steps will be clearer.

2. **Give your sales presentation and your pitch book to those buyers** - After executing confidentiality agreements, show off your business. Impress buyers with your company's historical growth, and give your sales pitch to drive up bids.

3. **Accept Indications of Interest (offers) from the buyers** - Buyers' Indications of Interest will provide you and your team a range for your business's sales price. Some buyers may offer $2 million to $4 million, while others bid between $10 million and $15 million. Their offers will indicate the valuation you can expect from your business.

4. **Answer buyer questions** - Next, give the buyers the chance to walk around your business and "kick the tires." Begin working with those who have offered the highest bids, and set up question and answer sessions with their teams. If you can answer their questions clearly and

concisely, they may present a higher final offer than their Indications of Interest said they would.

5. **Receive and accept a final offer** - After you have satisfactorily answered buyer questions, let your remaining few potential buyers make their final offers. If they are competing against one or two others, they may raise their bids higher than you expected. Accept the bid—the highest bid or the bid from the buyer you liked the most.

6. **Enter into final negotiations** - Once you have accepted ONE buyer's offer, let your exit team and their purchase team negotiate terms that will be advantageous to both parties.

7. **Close the deal** - Finally, get to the closing table, receive your check, and start the next phase of your life.

SELLING YOUR BUSINESS THROUGH A PRIVATE SALE

On the opposite side of the business auction lies the private sale. Auctions are not for every seller. Therefore, you might want to list your business through a private sale rather than through a less private auction if you meet one of the following qualifications:

1. Your business is a "small business" worth less than $7.5 million.

2. You have very little buyer interest.

3. You want to pitch a few people, not multiple people in multiple regions.

4. Your identified type of buyer is not comfortable with the auction process.

5. You are not comfortable with the auction process.

6. You have already identified a strategic buyer—a family member, an employee, a competitor, etc.

No matter which way you decide is the best way to sell your business, you probably already have interested buyers. You just have to figure out which particular process will get you the highest bid.

CHAPTER 32

PICK YOUR COMPENSATION METHOD

"Do your job and demand your compensation – but in that order."

Cary Grant

I f you are like me, you're probably worried about many things at this point in your business sale, especially money. With all the time, energy, and money you have invested into your business over the years and with all the money you are paying professionals to help you sell your business, how and when do *you* get paid? Deciding whether you want to offer your company for sale on the open auction market or to a smaller group of individuals is not the final decision you have to make before you list your business. By choosing how you want to be paid, you can minimize negative tax ramifications after the sale, and you can identify your business buyer more clearly before the sale.

#1 - CASH

The first way to sell your business is to sell it for cash. Most likely, this is the way you expect to get paid when you sell your company. Isn't cash king? Doesn't everyone like it? Of course you do. You have built and grown your company over years and years, and now you want that big, four-foot cardboard check presented to you, right?

I sold one of three businesses on a cash basis, and I felt like I had won the lottery! It was an outstanding experience, so if you are offered cash for your business, you can, "take the money and run." It's the easiest type of sales transaction, and it's the least risky one, too.

However, many times buyers do not want to outsource that much cash, so they will come up with other creative ways to fund, or buy, your business. Plus, you as a seller may not want to pay taxes on the capital gains you receive from the cash sale of your business. Therefore, you and your buyer may look for other buyout options.

#2 - STOCKS

Secondly, buyers and sellers can use one of two types of stock buyout methods to pay and to get paid at the closing of a business sale. For these stock methods to work, you must operate as a C Corporation or as an S Corporation (technically, an LLC taxed as a C or S Corp is also allowed) that can buy, sell, and trade company stock. Remember my discussion about business operations and entities in Chapter 4? This is one instance where your chosen entity can affect your future sellability.

An Employee Stock Ownership Plan (ESOP)

To get paid through an ESOP, you must hire an independent evaluator to place a value on your company's stock. Once the value is determined, you hire a trustee to set up and operate an independent trust. At that point, the trust buys stock shares from you based on the purchase price the evaluator set. Then, employees have the option to purchase company stock from the trust in the form of a retirement plan. When employees leave or retire, they can sell the stock back to the trust at a fair market value to cash out their retirement savings.

Although the ESOP can get very complicated, it has a lot of advantages. Essentially, this is a way an owner can remain with the company while taking capital out of the company. If you are not ready to retire or do not want to retire in the immediate future, you can set up an ESOP. Then, you can continue to run the organization until you are fully paid or have sold all your stock shares.

Another good thing about an ESOP is that it benefits and rewards long-term employees. The ESOP creates a long-term initiative and loyalty program that rewards employee commitment and hard work. It incentivizes employees

PICK YOUR COMPENSATION METHOD

to drive your company towards success because they own portions of it. The more valuable your stocks become, the more money they get when they sell!

An ESOP is not for every corporation, though. Some entrepreneurs don't like having a third party evaluate company shares. Many feel that the valuation is lower than what they would receive for their stocks on the open market. Another disadvantage of the ESOP is that the company must have cash. You have to keep a fair amount of cash on hand so that when employees leave, you can convert their stocks to cash and pay out their shares.

Stock Buyouts

This second method of stock buyouts can also get complicated, so I will try to make it as *financially simple* as possible. To generate additional capital or to retire from your business, you can sell company stocks. As in an ESOP, you want to hire an independent valuator to place a value on those stocks. Buyers can then purchase the majority of your shares, all of your shares, or portions of them. In doing so, they become shareholders/owners in your company and have rights to elect directors and vote on company policies. However, you have the option to keep some of the company's stock. Thus, you can maintain some control of the business AND receive immediate cash capital.

Let's assume the buying company or the majority shareholders drive the business to unprecedented success. Consequently, your shares increase in value, making you lots and lots of money. With hopes this will happen, you want to add a provision into the stock sale agreement that allows you to buy additional shares at set terms, such as at the price the shares were valued upon the sale of your business.

However, what if the purchasing company drives your company into the ground? What if the value of your stock plummets? You must have provisions written into the sales agreement which allow you to purchase additional shares at the same value majority owners can or which allow you to sell them to other owners at a predetermined set price.

Another provision you want to address in stock buyouts is a *tag-along right*. In other words, if buyers purchase the majority of your company shares for $10 and then find a buyer to pay $20 for them, make sure you can include your shares in that deal. You want to "tag-along" on that sale and get that $20 per share.

Lastly, make sure you address *piggyback rights* in a stock buyout. If the buying entity makes its shares public, you want the right to publicly register your shares, too. You want the right to "piggyback" on their success.

#3 - EARNOUT

I found the best definition of an earnout from Investopedia. The author explains that "an earnout is a contractual provision stating that the seller of a business is to obtain additional compensation in the future if the business achieves certain financial goals, which are usually stated as a percentage of gross sales or earnings."[48] Essentially, this allows the buyer to give you a fair price for your company now but gives you the bonus you think it's worth later if the business does well. Let's break that down.

Say your company has $5 million in sales and $500,000 in earnings. A buyer wants to pay $2.5 million for the company but you think that is too low. You personally believe the company's sales will drastically increase because of some groundwork you have laid. For both parties to agree on a sales transaction, you enter into an earnout, or a compromise. In this example, the seller pays the $2.5 million up front as a deposit on the business. Then, he agrees to give you the additional $2.5 million **IF** the company reaches $10 million in sales over a three-year period. If the company does not reach a certain amount of sales, the buyer does not have to pay you any additional money, or you can add in a provision that he will owe you "x" more dollars at the end of three years regardless of growth.

Using the same $5 million and $500,000 from our example, let's say the seller pays you $2.5 million upfront. Instead of asking for an additional $2.5 million **IF** the company reaches a certain amount of sales, you ask for a guaranteed 5 percent of the company's gross sales over the next three years. Then, if the business makes $10 million in three years, you get an additional

---

48 Investopedia. Earnout. (n.d.). Retrieved from https://www.investopedia.com/terms/e/earnout.asp

$500,000 per year for the three-year term. If the business makes $20 million, you earn another million per year of the three-year earnout term.

An earnout can offer buyers a handsome reward. It can also leave you with nothing other than the down payment. Buyers could put a novice in charge of your business who drives it into the ground. In three years, you get nothing else because the company closed or earned no profit. Similarly, buyers could have purchased your company to get rid of their competition. If they absorb your company into theirs or drive all your business to a sister company, then you get nothing other than the down payment. Therefore, be wary, and protect yourself. Know your buyers' intentions before you choose the earnout option.

#4 - SELLER-CARRIED NOTE

A great option for buyers, owner financing may not be the best option for you as a seller. Different than an earnout, you and the buyers agree on the company's worth. However, the buyers cannot or will not come up with the cash to cover the entire purchase price. The buyers will usually pay 65 to 80 percent of the company's value but will ask the seller to carry a promissory note for the remaining 20 to 35 percent. In this case, then, the buyers expect the seller to carry some of the risks with them.

If you are going to do a seller carry, take a few factors into consideration. Is your company well-seasoned? In other words, is it strong enough to withstand transitions within the market? Is your product or your service scalable and adaptable if technology advances or the economic market crashes? You may have jumped into a market fad. Maybe your company is one of 20 bakeries in a small town. Because of economic circumstance, the majority of those bakeries will close their doors. If you doubt the future longevity of your company for any reason, then you may want to choose a different buyout option.

Additionally, you must trust the buyers enough to carry a note. What happens if the buyers liquidate company assets or spend all the company cash? Can you trust them enough to make consistent, long-term payments to you? Essentially, you are leaving your greatest asset and all the company's assets at risk in buyers' hands. Talk with your legal team. If you agree to carry a note for the buyers, make sure you protect yourself within the sales agreement.

#5 - OFFER OF EMPLOYMENT

In this last option, buyers may offer you employment as part of the buyout. If you would like to sell but aren't ready to stop working, this option might work for you, or if the buyers want to purchase your company but don't know enough about your industry, they may ask you to remain in the company for a set amount of time to teach them how to operate the business. In my years as an exit planner, I have seen the offer of employment buyout work well, and I have seen it work poorly.

Sometimes, sellers stay to fulfill an employment contract and get frustrated. Usually, this happens when there is a significant age difference between the buyers and sellers. Other times, buyers and sellers may encounter personality conflicts. Remember, you have poured years of blood, sweat, and tears into this business and have made it your "own." If buyers come in and start making all kinds of changes to your "baby," their actions could make you resentful, angry, or bitter toward them.

If you and the buyers recognize that conflict can arise in this buyout option, you can build protective provisions into the employment contract. For instance, if buyers offer you employment and intend to become the President and the CEO of the company, you might ask that you report to them, not to a middleman. Also, make sure that the buyers spell out your specific role, your job description, and your work location. Lay everything on the table. The last thing you want to do is go from being the CEO of the company in Tennessee to cleaning toilets at a company located in Kansas (unless you like lots of farmland).

Nail down any "what-ifs" you can think of before your term of employment begins. What if you get fed up? Is there a fallback provision where you pay back some money, or do you get to leave and just give up some unearned compensation? What if the buyers get tired of you? Do they terminate you with pay? Without pay?

Outline everything. Determine your salary. Decide whether to place a salary cap on the buyers during your term of employment. Understand fringe benefits. Whatever you and the buyers do, seek legal advice to prepare for best and worst-case scenarios.

CHAPTER 33

MINIMIZE NEGATIVE TAX IMPLICATIONS

"The avoidance of taxes is the only intellectual pursuit that still carries any reward."

John Maynard Keynes

You must know that if money is changing hands, taxes follow. Sellers who understand that settling on a purchase price and a payout option is only the beginning of negotiations soon find themselves trying to minimize negative tax implications.

Overnight, many sellers become "armchair, Google tax experts" ready to take on the most knowledgeable tax planners...or so they think. If you research the internet for tax advice, you will learn a lot of information. However, that information may be completely inapplicable to you and your business sale. When you are dealing with taxes and sales negotiations related to the purchase agreement, be smart. Utilize the team you have built and assembled. Let the professionals identify ways you can reduce your tax burden upon the sale of your business.

Anytime you are dealing with taxes, talk to your Certified Public Accountant and your CERTIFIED FINANCIAL PLANNER™. What I have to say is not tax advice. Your circumstances will differ from mine and from my clients', so you need to consult your own CPA and CFP®. By working together, they can offer you the best tax advice based on your unique situation, so lean on them, and just use this chapter as a discussion starter.

THE TAX SEESAW EFFECT

During negotiations, your attorneys and the buyer's attorneys will be making changes to the language of the sale. Any time either of you make pertinent financial changes to the sales agreement (also known as the purchase agreement), one will face tax consequences, and the other will receive tax benefits. Changes in the purchase price, the payout, the earnout, the type of sale, or combinations thereof directly affect tax liabilities each party will face. When your teams work to clarify the language of the sale, you will see a seesaw effect in tax credits and debits. Rather than giving some and taking some, you will win some and lose some. The more taxes the buyer pays, the less you pay or vice-versa. There is no win-win. One party will "win" the battle to minimize taxes while the other will "lose."

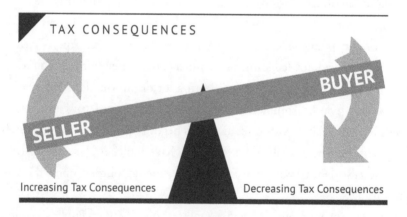

Typically, the IRS taxes earnings from the sale of intangible assets (i.e. goodwill) and certain tangible assets (i.e. company stock) at a Long-Term Capital Gains rate of 15 to 20 percent. On the other hand, the IRS typically taxes earnings from the sale of tangible assets like equipment and accounts receivable at a higher Ordinary Income rate of 25 to 40 percent (the actual percentage rates sellers pay depends on their income bracket and the current depreciation schedule).

Thus, in a business sale, you as a seller hope to increase the percentage buyers pay for assets which generate the lowest tax rates for you and decrease the percentage buyers pay for assets which generate higher tax rates for you. Buyers hope to do the exact opposite to take advantage of depreciation and/or amortization on hard assets to minimize their own immediate and future tax liabilities.

As you can see, your goals and your buyer's goals directly oppose one another. The seesaw cannot reach a level plane; it must tip up toward one party and down toward another. Whether you sell your company's assets or its stock, you will have to pay taxes, but your goal as seller is to minimize your tax implications upon the sale of your business.

THE ASSET SALE

In an asset sale, you retain possession of the legal entity but nothing more. Essentially, you are selling your company's tangible and intangible assets, but you are not giving up your company's name or its liabilities. Sometimes, you can retain your cash on hand and accounts receivable, too.

Generally, self-employed medical professionals participate in asset sales because the small business operates under the proprietor's name. If you are a dentist, chiropractor, physical therapist, optometrist, or the like and practice as "Jane Smith Clinic," then your buyer will purchase your assets but not your identifying name.

Looking at the tax seesaw effect, an asset sale can place you in the "losing" position. Let's say that furniture, equipment, and patient bases make up most of your sellable assets. As I have already mentioned, earnings from the sale of tangible assets usually fall within the Ordinary Income Tax rates of 25 to 40 percent. Goodwill (the value of your company not attached to a tangible asset) makes up a very small percentage of assets within the purchase price. Likely, earnings from the sale of that intangible asset will fall within the Long-Term Capital Gains Tax rates of 15 to 20 percent.

In this case, you the seller could pay the higher Ordinary Income Tax rates on the majority of your earnings from the sale, so if you are selling assets for $1 million, you could pay upwards of $400,000 in federal taxes, and that number doesn't even account for state and local taxes you will owe! (Of course, this is a hypothetical situation. The exact details of your situation could vary greatly.)

On the other hand, with a little tax planning, you could tip your seesaw the other way. You could reallocate the sales contract to be mostly self-generated goodwill with the equipment carrying a much lower weight on the sales contract. In this potential situation, you could pay Long-Term Capital Gains Tax rates for that majority intangible asset at 15 to 20 percent. Then, you could pay higher tax rates on the minority earnings from the sale of your tangible assets. In this case, you would win the seesaw negotiations because you virtually receive the tax rate of a stock sale (see below).

THE STOCK SALE

In a stock sale, the buyer purchases your ownership stock in the company. The buyer assumes ownership of the entity, the name, the assets, and *all the liabilities*. Do not miss that…you just sold your liabilities!!! THIS IS HUGE!!!

As I already mentioned, company stock is often taxed at a Long-Term Capital Gains rate of 15 to 20 percent rather than at the Ordinary Income rate of 25 to 40 percent. Depending on the sales price and your individual income bracket, you might even get away with paying zero taxes on this type of sale.

THE PREDETERMINED SALE

However, you may not be able to participate in a stock sale, and you may not be able to tweak your tax liability percentages. Yet again, your structural entity selection affects your business's sale because your company only has stock ownership (or membership interest in the case of an LLC) to sell if you operate as a C Corporation, an S Corporation, or an LLC. If you operate as a sole proprietor or general partnership, you have no ownership/membership interest to sell. Thus, you will sell your assets and pay tax liabilities on those earnings based on your tangible and intangible asset percentages.

Similarly, if you operate your company as a C Corporation, that entity choice predetermined your tax liabilities years before you ever got to this point of a business sale. The government taxes C Corporations AND C Corp shareholders yearly in what we call a double taxation liability. That same double taxation status applies to the company's sale as well. Your company will pay taxes on its sales earnings, AND shareholders will pay taxes on the same earnings, so long before you ever sell your company, decisions you make can affect the taxes you pay on your sales earnings. Therefore, you should employ a good CERTIFIED FINANCIAL PLANNER™ and a good Certified Public Accountant when you first decide to sell your business, years before you get to the actual sale. Pick professionals who deal with business and tax planning because, quite possibly, they can save you thousands or millions of dollars in taxes.

PRE-PLANNING CAN MINIMIZE THE NEGATIVE TAX IMPLICATIONS

Many times, depending on your age or your overarching goals, a little bit of charitable planning as it relates to your business sale or a few slight adjustments could save you lots of money. A sale I was working on when I wrote the blog post "Achieving Charitable Desires While Increasing Your Net Gain" provides a great example of this.[49]

Clients of mine stood to gross about $10 million upon the sale of their company. Before the sale took place, the owners told those of us on their exit team that they wanted to give $1 million of their proceeds to a religious charity. First, we verified that the organization fell under the IRS's qualified charity rules and regulations. Then, we looked at the clients' tax implications.

Originally, the clients hoped to donate the money *after* they sold the business, so we ran an analysis based on that scenario. If they sold the business for $10 million, paid their taxes, and donated the money after the fact, they would walk away with approximately $7.27 million net cash. Since $1 million would

---

49 Goodbread, Justin. Achieving Charitable Desires While Increasing Your Net Gain. (August 2017). Retrieved from https://financiallysimple.com/achieving-charitable-desires-while-increasing-your-net-gain/

go to charity, we determined that they would lose around $2.8 million of their $10 million deal.

Alternatively, we did an analysis based on a pre-gift scenario. If the owners gave a gift of ownership in the company to charity before the sale ever took place, they would net approximately $7.5 million cash. That is over $200,000 more in the owners' pockets with just a little bit of planning!

Besides charitable giving, the timing of your business's sale can make a difference in your tax liabilities. If your tax liabilities will be $1 million and you close the sale in December, you will owe that money by April 15. However, you could delay the closing by one month, and you would not owe that $1 million until the following April. What if you took that $1 million you owe the government and invested it in a low-risk CD or savings account for those 15 months? You would make money off the government's money.

Small changes in buyer allocation percentages can also make a difference in your tax liabilities. If you increase the percentage allocated to intangible assets and decrease the percentage allocated to tangible assets, you could minimize your tax liabilities.

Those charitable contributions or small adjustments are just a taste of how tax planning can help you. Tax planning with a CFP® and a CPA years before you sell your business can potentially save you hundreds of thousands of dollars, so don't wait until you cash out of your business to look at your tax implications. Look now! Then, keep as much of your earnings as possible when you sell!

LIST YOUR BUSINESS FOR SALE

"The only way around is through."

Robert Frost

A fter 10 years of grunt work preparing your business for sale, you have begun preparing your personal finances and your emotional self for the sale, too. The time to list your beloved business for sale is now. Do not wait any longer. With the help of your advisory team members and business team members, gather your essential documents, and go "sell" your business to your identified potential buyers. Decide how you want to sell, and begin the process. While the actual sales process will not take years like your value acceleration did, it could still take upwards of a year, so let's get started!

CHAPTER 34

IDENTIFY YOUR BUYER

*"Making a company fit to sell may be the only way
to ensure you never need a buyer."*

Margaret Heffernan

Now that you and your exit team (particularly you and your sales facilitator) have chosen a sales arena and a method of compensation that best minimizes your tax ramifications, you can identify the type of buyer most likely to buy your business and list your business for sale in that marketplace. For instance, if you are selling your assets to a private buyer, you might offer your company to a family member or to an employee before you advertise on the open market. Yet, if you want to sell your stock shares in an international market, you may market to a capital investor.

THE CHRISTMAS SUIT

On the day after Christmas last year, my mom and I went to Walmart. As we walked in the door, we came face-to-face with a clearance area, and on one of those racks was a *hideous* suit. I can't even begin to tell you how ugly this suit was. It was a man's formal dress suit with pants, blazer, shirt, and tie all in Christmas green with Christmas icons plastered *all over it*! Every other square inch of the fabric on the entire suit was covered in elves, Santas, presents, Christmas trees, and gingerbread men. From top to bottom, people. The pants, the tie, the blazer, the belt. I mean, *it was hideous*.

As I was looking at this thing kind of cockeyed, I said to my mom, "There is NO WAY on God's green earth I'd be caught dead in a suit that looked like that." Mom, being the wonderful Southern woman she is, replied, "Well, different strokes for different folks, Son."

IT TAKES ALL TYPES OF BUSINESS BUYERS

My mom was right, you know? Life would be boring if we were all the same, right? Personally, I'm glad we're not all the same. We all have different likes and dislikes, different preferences and tastes. It takes all of us to make the world go 'round.

Similarly, business buyers, like business sales facilitators, come in all different shapes and sizes. Some buyers have a little bit of money while others have a lot. Frugality rules some while "spend it if you have it" rules others. Some may want an instant return on their investment while others do not really care about getting a return. Other buyers may look at the potential Long-Term Capital Gain they would receive from buying your business while others may want to eliminate their competition.

Who, then, are the business buyers? What type of person or company buys businesses? Well, buyers tend to fall into a couple different categories, and by going through the following exercise, you can identify your potential buyer, especially now that you have hired a sales facilitator. Once you and your advisory team understand who your buyer is, then you can design, shape, and create your sales campaign to appeal to that type of business buyer.

THE LOW-RISK BUYERS

The first major category of buyers consists of two very different types of business customers who both desire low-risk purchases:

1. The Financial Buyer

First, we have the individuals who trade businesses like they trade stock. These people will crunch numbers to estimate their return on investment in every type of detailed scenario. Oftentimes, these buyers are looking to hold the business for less than 10 years. Thus, they will want to know all the ins and outs of your business. They are NOT taking any risk that they will not make a return on their investment within a very short time period.

Not all financial buyers are number crunchers or business traders, though. Some financial buyers come in the form of family members or employees who purchase the company. They may want to grow the company and sell it within 10 years, so they will not be taking risks and gambling on precarious investments. They will look to earn a sizable living by continuing the company you began. Then, they will hope to sell for profit when they want to retire or go on to the next great thing for their lives.

2. The Strategic Buyer

Now, strategic buyers are just a slight bit different. These individuals are not looking to flip a business, per se. Rather, they are looking to buy a business which enhances their own. They may want to add a cog to their business wheel that will work in harmony with their current company. For instance, if they repair water lines, they might want to acquire a boring company or a paving company. Both of these companies could add synergy to the buyers' current utility company. Or, buyers may choose to merge with a company that repairs roads to fix the holes their company creates.

However, not all strategic buyers want to add harmonious pieces to their existing business. Some may be your competitors, looking to take over your customer base or your market niche. They want harmony; they just acquire it by "getting rid of" their competition.

THE HIGH-RISK BUYERS

The second category of business buyers breaks into three different high-risk takers, if you will. These are the gamblers of the purchasing world.

1. The Angel Investor

Angel investors typically work with startup companies that show promise but have no proven track record. Therefore, they take the most risk. These investors come in, buy part or all the company, and help drive its success. Whenever they purchase or buy-in to a business, they usually do not take all the assets or buy all of the stock. However, they will take a majority interest in the company.

2. The Venture Capitalist

Venture capitalists are not going to buy companies at ground level. Think ABC's *Shark Tank* here. These multimillionaires will buy into a company or take ownership of a company that has a proven track record of success but needs connections that only the venture capitalist can provide. The venture capitalists hope that their high-level affiliations will drive the company to exponential success, making them even more money.

3. The Private Equity Firms

Private equity firms are a bit different from the other investors because they typically only purchase the best of the best of the best companies. Consequently, they pay the most and typically deal with the largest companies worth over $100 million. These firms are looking to buy the next Google or Amazon.

LOCATION MATTERS TO POTENTIAL BUSINESS BUYERS

Besides identifying the type of risk-taker likely to buy your company, you have to look at your location. In other words, your local, regional, national, or global size can determine which types of business buyers will be attracted to your company.

Those companies that operate in a small, localized area will normally seek "mom-and-pop" purchasers. The buyers' goal is to come in and get a return on their investment within about three to five years. They are not particularly interested in spending a long time getting a company off the ground, so they seek an established business they can purchase for hundreds of thousands or a few million dollars. Then, they expect to recoup their investment in a short amount of time.

Regional purchasers will typically buy companies that operate in larger arenas that have mastered the art of scalability. These buyers will purchase companies with multiple storefronts in multiple cities and states. Because of the bigger investment and the larger marketplace, regional purchasers expect to wait about five to 10 years before they see a return on their initial investment.

National and/or international buyers will purchase the publicly traded or globally based companies. These investors look for companies that are the "best of the best." Paying more than local and regional buyers, they want everything the company has to offer. With such a large investment, these buyers will insist on solid profits from the very beginning, so they will look at purchasing companies that show reliable trends and a steady customer base.

THE BUYER IS YOUR ULTIMATE CUSTOMER

Now that you are ready to sell your business, identifying your potential buyer will help clarify where you will look for investors and how you will reach them. Ideally, you want to attract a buyer who will agree to your asking price.

CHAPTER 35

PREPARE YOUR PITCH BOOK

"An entrepreneur must pitch a potential investor
for what the company is worth as well as
sell the dream on how much of a profit can be made."

Daymond John

I t's finally time to get your business sold! You have all members of your team assembled, you have decided where and how to sell your business, and you know where to look for potential buyers. Your goal at this point is to list your business for sale and to highlight the value you have built within your business to attract those buyers. After selling products or services within your business all these years, you are about to make the most important sales pitch of your life. Therefore, you need to enter the sales arena with a well assembled pitch book in hand.

WHAT IS A BUSINESS PITCH BOOK?

Also commonly referred to as a play book, your pitch book is a collection of written documents and printed reports that provide your potential buyer with the relevant details of your company. That's all it is. Honestly, it looks remarkably like your original business plan and will even include many excerpts from it, but it functions as your company's "brag book" rather than its blueprints. If it's well-written and well-constructed, your pitch book will have buyers salivating at the opportunity to make you an offer because they want your valuable business.

Since every company is different, your exit team will offer advice for what you need to include in your pitch book. Most business pitch books, though, will include five major categories:

1. The history of your company

2. Your existing team players

3. Your business model

4. The company's current financial situation

5. Your financial forecast

If you created your original business plan and have reevaluated it and revised it each year, compiling this information will not be hard; you already have it. All you must do is synthesize and summarize the information in a way that will show-off the hard work you and your team members have done throughout the years. However, if you haven't written an original business plan or kept up with revisions, gathering and writing this information will be hard work. At times, it will even feel tedious and futile. Yet, if you take the time to do it right, the pitch book's existence could bring you offers from multiple buyers and a desired, fair price for your company.

KEEP A RUNNING PRO FORMA

For me, writing my pitch book is an ongoing process. I want my entire company outlined in such a way that IF the time comes or WHEN the time comes, I do not have to create the book from scratch. I always want my pitch book ready just as I want my business plan up-to-date . I want them to work together to make my business a valuable, sellable commodity.

Yet, why would I advise you to go through the exercise of recording your company's history while you are still making its history? Why would I tell you to keep a running pro forma throughout the years you are building the value in your business?

Well, like I discussed in Chapter 6, the pro forma helps you communicate where you want to take your company, and it provides a nice trail guide of where you have been and what has worked for you over the years. By downloading Profit and Loss Statement categories into a pro forma at the end of each year, you can evaluate your historic income growth and clearly see how much the company's income has grown over the past four or five years.

Once you see your actual growth rate over the years, you can make realistic predictions about your future financial growth. If your revenue has grown at a 10 percent annual rate, you cannot realistically project a 30 percent yearly growth rate in your pitch book unless you make drastic changes. However, if your updated pro forma shows that you have maintained a historic growth rate of 10 percent, and you now project a 9 percent future growth rate, that should be easy to obtain. Potential buyers can easily "buy into" that calculation.

HOW TO COMPILE A PITCH BOOK

If you are ready to sell your business now, and you have not maintained a business plan and kept a running pro forma, how do you accomplish this monumental project? Where do you start? Here are a few ideas to help you get started on your pitch book, but remember that you will need to modify these suggestions to meet your individual needs:

- Designate a team member to compile and edit all the necessary information.

- Write down or record your own memories of your company's history, including highlights and low times.

- Ask your team players to write autobiographies.

- Have your management team outline your business model.

- Ask your accountant or accounting team to create, update, or print your pro forma.

As you create your pitch book, do not get too caught up in every word because there will be many changes. Your exit team will make changes and modify your text. Your advisor will craft in the keywords that will catch a buyer's eye. They know how to do it, so trust them.

When you build the pitch book, you obviously want to present your company in the best light possible. You want to show historical *growth*. Ideally, you will show-off your advisory team members and your business's team members. You will also outline an "enviable business model" and illustrate your company's current "stable" financials. However, do NOT make preventable mistakes. Two decisions you make could cost you the entire sale of your business, so avoid making them.

- Do NOT inflate your financial forecast - If you make your forecast overly optimistic, buyers could delay the sales process to make sure your company reaches its projected success. If it fails to meet predictions, buyers could significantly lower their offers or walk away from the sale altogether, so be conservatively realistic.

- Do NOT give away the keys to your company's success - Some potential buyers would love to get their hands on your pitch book to learn your company's secrets. If you provide them with your company's data without asking them to sign non-disclosure or non-compete agreements, you could lose your business sale and possibly your actual business to a competitor, so rely on your legal team to protect your investment from nefarious individuals.

A good business pitch book can be judged only after you have received the desired, fair price offer for your business, so have you started compiling the information for your pitch book yet? If you have not, why don't you start? If you are sitting across the table from potential buyers making a sales presentation, your pitch book is there to help you make the most important sale of your life.

CHAPTER 36

MAKE YOUR SALES PRESENTATION

"Luck is a matter of preparation meeting opportunity."

Lucius Annaeus Seneca

With the necessary tools in hand, you are ready to make the greatest sales pitch of your life. Years of hard work culminate in this moment, so your business sales presentation must be flawless for potential buyers to see your company the way you see it. This is where you put the "sales into the sale." You want to do such a good job presenting your company to potential buyers that they will make you an offer, and a fair offer at that.

AN EXIT TEAM ARMY

I have sat on both sides of the business sales table. If you remember, I've already sold three businesses of my own, but as a CERTIFIED FINANCIAL PLANNER™, I have also helped countless clients sell their companies or purchase companies. In fact, one business sale stands out in my mind.

Early in my career, some 15 to 20 years ago, I acted as a financial advisor for a client looking to buy a business. When my client's team and I sat down across from the seller, we were impressed by the "army" she had assembled. I mean, professionals and her top managers filled the whole side of her table. She was *ready* to convince my client that her company was worth his money.

I will never forget what I learned that day. During a break in the business sales presentation, the buyer, his CPA, and I sat in the hallway talking about what we had just experienced. As we mulled over the seller's pitch, the seasoned

CPA addressed us and said, "Boys, if we end up liking this company, we have to move fast. The buyer has made a big mistake."

Young and naive, I blurted out, "A mistake?! Dude, she's got an army with her!" Yet, this CPA continued, "Nope. She's put her top employees at the table." I can still remember looking at him like a calf looking at a new gate. "Why is this a mistake?" was the only question I could verbalize. I just could not put it together.

If you are like I was, you're probably wondering why having the buyer's best employees at the sales presentation table was a mistake. If you've gotten to the point where you are actually selling your business, don't you need the team members with you who have helped you reach this finish line?

Well, let's think about it. If you have followed my advice in this book, you have hired a good CFP®, a good attorney, and a good CPA. You may even have hired some transition experts and a valuation expert. Sure, you've built a great team, but what happens next? You go into your company and grab your division heads—your CFO, your CEO, and your department managers. You probably think that your team will handle the sales presentation and the due diligence period that follows with you. After all, you need the best-of-the-best putting in the MANY hours required to bring this sale to the "payout" you desire.

While your professional advisors respond to the buyer's questions, your company leaders are left scrambling about, trying to keep up with requested documents, guided tours, phone calls, and any other whim of the buyer's team during that extensive due diligence period. Yet, the rest of your company's team members are left unattended for the many hours, days, and months your team leaders are preparing for and attending these meetings. Performance falls. Customers leave. Revenue plummets.

Because you pulled out your business's leaders—the people who run the company—your business begins to suffer. That can be devastating, and it could cost you your biggest "client." You could lose some of your best employees. Heaven help you, you could even lose some of the key players on your transition team, and don't think for a second that the buyer doesn't recognize what is happening. He does. He will, and he could possibly end up walking away, leaving you to pick up the pieces of what is left of your company.

KEEP SELLING

While you may think that pulling your best team members into your business sales presentation and the following due diligence period is a good idea, it could cost your sale. The CPA I worked with all those years ago recognized the mistake the seller made. He recognized that her company could suffer from her actions.

What do you do, then, to avoid making this rookie mistake? Well, you hire consultants and non-critical personnel. Long before you reach this presentation point, you are going to hire and train people to learn your management systems. You will teach them how every department in your company operates so these consultants can either come to the business table with you or keep the company running smoothly while your original team members come with you. Your goal is to keep operations running in such a way that your company's worth does not diminish during its sales process.

Yes, you will have to spend some extra money but as my CPA friend told me, "I can calculate the expense of hiring the employees that we need. What I can't calculate is the potential devastation of making this rookie mistake."

NAIL YOUR BUSINESS SALES PRESENTATION

Once you shore up your company's health and well-being, it's time to make your sales pitch! You are going to have to try to sell the company so that an actual sale takes place. Your sales pitch must be so strong that it persuades the buyer to make you an offer. More than that, you want the buyer to offer what the valuation advisor has told you your company is worth.

Remember, the buyers' teams are ready, too. They are sitting across the table with a red pen, taking notes, waiting to get a toe-hold in the cracks of your business sales presentation. They know your company is valuable, but they want to find reasons to offer you a lower price to save themselves money. So how do you prevent cracks from showing during your business sales presentation?

1. **Choose well-spoken presenters** - Whether this is you or other members of your team, make sure you have speakers who are good on

their feet. Make sure they can answer most of the questions about your business or return with answers to questions they do not know.

2. **Practice, practice, practice** - Have the speakers make the presentation repeatedly to multiple groups of people before the actual sales pitch. Test their company knowledge and their ability to respond to questions quickly and competently.

3. **Answer the questions** - Ensure your speakers will answer the buyers' questions truthfully and succinctly. You don't want speakers giving 10-minute answers to two-second questions. That just leaves room and time for more cracks to show that were not even addressed. Also, don't let your speakers talk around the answers. Make sure they respond honestly if they don't know the answer but ensure they are reliable enough to get back to the team once they find an answer.

4. **Pitch an unranked team** - Find buyers looking for a business *unlike* yours, and pitch your sale to them and their teams for feedback. Let your transition team take notes, too, during the presentation so that you can make corrections to the pitch based on constructive feedback.

5. **Bring your A game.** Don't wait until the night before your sales presentation to prepare. Be wise. Get plenty of sleep the night before, and wake up early enough not to be rushed or stressed the morning of the pitch. You have one shot at your top prospect, so you must make the best presentation you possibly can.

You have done an amazing job getting your company to this point, so I know you can do this, too!

NEGOTIATE THE SALE

"Let us never negotiate out of fear. But let us never fear to negotiate."
John F. Kennedy

O nce you receive an offer from a potential buyer, you begin a new
phase in the sales process—negotiations.

CHAPTER 37

RECEIVE AN OFFER

"The reward for work well done is the opportunity to do more."
Jonas Salk

After listening to your sales presentation, one or several of your *potential* buyers might become *intentional* buyers. If buyers see value in your business, they can issue a Letter of Intent to purchase your company. Negotiations begin. One of my attorney friends calls this stage the "first of many battles" in the "war you're going to wage." If buyer and seller teams reach agreements beneficial to both parties, you win the first battle in the formal business sale.

As I have done before, let me implore you to listen to your professional legal counsel. Rely on your exit team to guide you through the landmines. This is an exciting time! However, don't let the thrill of a Letter of Intent to buy your business cost you. Take the first step in the formal business sale cautiously.

BUTTERFLIES IN MY STOMACH

Do you remember your elementary school antics? Like any kid, my friends and I had childhood crushes and chased girls on the playground. Inevitably, some of my friends even handed girls the "Do you like me?" letter. You know the one I am talking about—the one that asks you to check "Yes" or "No."

Maybe you didn't participate in that "nonsense," but you do remember the first time you asked someone out. Surely, I wasn't the only one with butterflies in my stomach. Will she say yes? What if she says no? Then, she said, "Yes," and it was like a weight was lifted off my shoulders. That feeling is one-of-a-kind excitement and relief that you just don't forget.

I have only experienced that same type of feeling during one other circumstance in my life—the day I received my first Letter of Intent. Years after those silly elementary school days and after I met the woman of my dreams, I decided to relocate to Tennessee. I knew that I couldn't take my landscaping company with me. Since I had a business partner, I went to him and proposed that he buy out my half of the company. After talking with his wife, he came back and gave me a Letter of Intent to buy my part of the business. I will never forget it. It was awesome, just like the feeling I had back in grade school when I asked a girl to go out with me!

THE PURPOSE OF THE LETTER OF INTENT

Sometimes called a Memorandum of Understanding or an LOI, the Letter of Intent alerts a business seller that a buyer "intends" to purchase his company. Usually, the LOI is non-binding, but many courts across our nation and around the world uphold its provisions as contractual and binding. Therefore, whenever you receive a Letter of Intent, contact your attorney and your exit team. Let them review the document and guide your next steps.

In its most basic form, the LOI is an agreement to agree or to reach an agreement. Just like a first date sets the stage for a relationship, the Letter of Intent sets the stage for your business sale. It can effectively do one or more of the following things:

- Lay out the expectations and essential terms of the business sale.

- Serve as preliminary documentation for lenders or governmental boards.

- Put the public on notice that there will be a sales transaction.

- Determine which party or which team member will draft certain documents.

- Set a time for due diligence, negotiations, purchasing exclusivity, purchase agreements, and closings.

ELEMENTS OF A LETTER OF INTENT

Whether the Letter of Intent shows a basic commitment between the buyer and seller or publicizes the trading of a company's stock, it will inevitably contain several elements. While not exhaustive, I have compiled a list of details attorneys I work with and I have seen throughout the years.

A Letter of Intent will include some or all of the following:

- A list of the assets to be sold in the transaction

- The purchase price for the business and all its stated assets

- A good faith, or earnest money, deposit

- Exclusivity period parameters

- Expected length of time for due diligence to occur

- Signed confidentiality agreements

- Definitions of important terms that might be used during the transaction

- A target date for the execution of the purchase agreement

- Allocation of expenses for both parties

- Identification of a sale's jurisdiction and governing entities

Since the Letter of Intent signals the start of the formal business sales process, you must be more cautious than ever before. Buyers will make many demands, and you have the choice to accept them or refuse them. Adding restrictions or limits to buyer demands can protect your business during this due diligence period but remember to lean on the exit team you have assembled to make wise decisions.

When I receive a Letter of Intent on behalf of my clients or when I have sold my own businesses, I typically follow certain guidelines. Most likely, your exit team will follow similar ones. Nonetheless, here are the guidelines I tend to follow:

- Limit the exclusivity period to 90 days - If you have been properly preparing to sell your business, you should have most of the data the buyer will request ready. By limiting the time you give this particular buyer exclusive rights to buy your business, you prevent the buyer from dragging out the process so long that other buyers lose interest in case this one dissolves.

- Request the delivery of a purchase agreement within 60 days - Dragging out the sales process could keep you from effectively managing your company which could cause the value of your company to decrease over time. The buyer could then leverage that to lower his purchase price.

- Keep other Letters of Intent you receive private - If you receive other Letters of Intent during the due diligence process with the first buyer, keep them to yourself, especially if the offers are lower than the one you are working to finalize. You don't want the buyer to lower his purchase price to match other ones.

- Do not take responsibility for all fees - Don't give the buyer everything and the kitchen sink! Share responsibility for legal fees and professional fees incurred during this time.

- List everything that is not included in the sale - Just as you list everything that is included in the sale, be sure to list everything you are taking with you, what is NOT included in the sale. If you want to keep a piece of equipment or a plaque on the wall, list it. Do not be afraid to keep things you need to live your life after the sale. Just be sure to clarify what you are keeping versus what you are selling.

- Address what will happen to cash on hand and Accounts Receivable - Clarify whether the seller is buying any, some, or all rights to your cash on hand and your accounts receivable. Have a plan in place for the buyer to purchase the 30-day, 60-day, or 90-day+ accounts. Maybe have them buy the current accounts at a dollar-for-dollar rate. Then, maybe sell the outstanding 60-day+ accounts for 50 cents on the dollar and the 90-day+ accounts for 10 cents on the dollar. You don't have to include any of this in the sale, but you do need to spell out what will be done with those open accounts and excess cash.

- Be wary of formula pricing - Also known as cap pricing, formula pricing places a set cap on the sales price. While this may work if a buyer has offered you top dollar for your company, it usually keeps a seller from negotiating a higher sales price as the seller finds more value in the company.

- Do not text or email without attorney approval - Since this is the beginning of a FORMAL business sale, any and all written communication can affect the terms of your Letter of Intent. Do not send out a "quick text" or a raging email without consulting your team because that "quick text" or that rampaging email could alter the course of your sale.

- Refuse to accept IOUs - If you agree to a promissory note for the cash on hand or the accounts receivable, the seller could receive it all, spend it all, and leave town without giving you a dime. Don't trust someone you don't know with millions of dollars. Work those accounts into your deal so that the seller will not owe you money AFTER you sell.

A sharp buyer is going to try to get everything he can, so when you are dealing with the Letter of Intent to buy your business, listen to your legal and professional counsel. While this process is probably new to you, they have dealt with this before, so seek and follow advice. Be excited, but be wise.

Receiving a Letter of Intent is a major event. You are going to feel butterflies of excitement and fear in your chest. It's almost like hitting the business lottery.

Now is when your business deal is going to make it or break it. If you can make it through to the end, though, the payout is totally worth it.

CHAPTER 38

AVOID MISTAKES

"A smart man makes a mistake, learns from it, and never makes that mistake again. But a wise man finds a smart man and learns from him how to avoid the mistake altogether."

Roy H. Williams

If you have systematically prepared and compiled documents, reports, business plans, and pitch books over the 10 years or so that you prepared your business for sale, the formal business sale could happen within a period of weeks or months. In comparison to 10 years, that's no time at all! If you do not slow things down, mistakes you make in the business sales process could cost you hundreds of thousands or even millions of dollars, and of course, there are no redos after all is said and done.

NO MULLIGANS ALLOWED

As part of my Turf Grass Management degree courses at Abraham Baldwin Agricultural College in South Georgia, I was able to play a ton of golf. I have played at all the Sea Island courses, several Fazio courses, and even at TPC Saw Grass the week after a pro tour went through the course. As much as I would try to play like Tiger Woods, I would inevitably have to say, "Let me use my Mulligan on that one."

I can specifically remember hole 17 at Saw Grass. When we reached this iconic hole, my group decided to try and match Tiger Woods to see how good we really were. I grabbed my pitching wedge like Tiger, but my ball fell way short. I eventually did get a ball to land on the green with a 7 iron, but when I went to putt, the greens were so fast that I overshot the hole and my ball went right into the water. Moral of the story…Tiger is pretty awesome! I think I ended up using 11 Mulligans on the one hole that day!

However, I never had to use a Mulligan in a do-or-die situation that could cost me millions of dollars of prize money. Personal restraint on the golf course was not required because I had nothing to lose, so I used Mulligans like golfers drank water on muggy Georgia days.

However, there are no redos at this point in the game. You do not get a Mulligan. The single hardest thing you will face at the time of business sale negotiations is personal restraint. However, moving too quickly or acting based on emotions may cause you to make irrational decisions that become permanent disasters and mistakes.

Buyers are not personally invested in your business's exit and valuation, but you are. When you list your business for sale, the majority of your personal worth is most likely tied up in your company. Thus, selling it will be hard, scary, and emotionally exhausting. You do not want a perceptive buyer to interpret your up and down emotions as weakness, though. Demonstrating a half-hearted attempt to sell your company at your asking price during negotiations could prove devastating, so you need to stay strong and fight for the price you have already determined you need.

NEGOTIATION DOS AND DON'TS

Once you receive a buyer's offer, you can do several things to exude an air of confidence you may not feel. You don't want to walk into negotiations with weak knees and ask for a Mulligan after you fall on your face. Therefore, what can you do to ensure a successful sale happens?

DO:

1. **Have courage** - Pull yourself up by the bootstraps, and man up! The minute you receive an offer, jump in or stay out.

2. **Contact your Certified Exit Planning Advisor** - If you have not already, now is the time to contact a Certified Exit Planning Advisor.

3. **Choose a Chief Operating Exit Planning Officer** - Choose one of your advisory team members to oversee the sale and negotiation process with precision. Designate a Chief Operating Exit Planning Officer to orchestrate the players, call the game shots, and bring in special teams if necessary.

As you and your team members prepare to show a strong, united front in the face of your intentional buyer, you don't want to make rookie mistakes.

DON'T:

1. Stop working on your business.

2. Take any offer just because it's the first offer.

3. Get over-eager to sell.

4. Quit in the middle.

Selling a business is hard, and the fittest person in the competition usually wins. After buyers make an offer, they are going to try to wear you down to get you to cut your sales price or to change your terms. Just stay diligent. When your stamina wavers, depend on your advisory team to stay strong during negotiations.

Most of all, remember that you don't get to mess up now and call a Mulligan. If you make mistakes during negotiations, you could end up losing hundreds of thousands if not millions of dollars. You could end up never selling the business or selling it for less than you need. There are a lot of dangers here, so whenever you enter the negotiation process, jump in wholeheartedly, and follow some of the helpful points I listed.

CHAPTER 39

PERFORM DUE DILIGENCE

"Obviously, there's the temptation to sit back and smile, ...But there's so much at stake, we have to do our due diligence."

Ralph Neas

After the buyer issues a Letter of Intent and while both sets of team members are drafting a sales agreement, you will enter into a period of due diligence. This is perhaps one of the most stressful periods of a formal business sale for the seller because the buyer will be trying to figure out why your company is not worth what you think it's worth. The buyer is intentionally digging up dirt on your business while you are trying to remain calm under pressure.

BABY ON BOARD

One of the funniest examples of due diligence I can remember came in the form of a baby seat purchase. Some of my dear friends were expecting their first baby, and Daddy was bound and determined that only the best car seat would do for his new "peanut."

For months, my friend exercised the due diligence process. He went online and found specifics about every car seat currently on the market. Then, he built an Excel spreadsheet around the information. He categorized each and every feature of the seat—ease of use, restraint, band width, type of fabric, etc.

He didn't even stop there! He actually purchased all three top car seats he identified from his spreadsheet and put them through his own type of product testing, going as far as throwing each seat down a mountain with a doll strapped in its restraints. As you can imagine, I gave him a hard time over the entire thing.

PREPARE FOR THE BUYER'S DUE DILIGENCE

Whether you have thought about it this way or not, you perform due diligence just about every day, and you can bet your britches that your business buyer will conduct his due diligence after he has given you a Letter of Intent. As standard procedure, buyers will ask you for sets of business and financial documents they want their team to review, and they will ask you a myriad of questions about your business. Even after you provide the documents and answer their questions, buyers will ask you for more information.

Most likely, your buyers will also send their advisory teams in to review the different areas of your business. Those team members will research your operations, your sales, your marketing, your finances, and your deliveries. They may even ask to speak to your key employees, and after all of that, the buyers will continue to quiz you about everything they have learned thus far in the process. Remember, the buyers' goal is to show you how ugly your business is so that they don't have to pay full price for it.

The due diligence process can make or break your business's final sale, so how are you to approach it? Well, you can do one or all of the following six things to make the due diligence process a little less stressful:

1. **Anticipate buyer requests and prepare.**

   To anticipate what buyers will request from you, write out a list of everything you would want to know about your business if you were the buyer. Then, compile, organize, and prepare the documents, reports, and data for the buyers' team.

   Remember, preparation is part of this equation. Anticipation without preparation only increases your stress level when you are working with deadlines and big money. Having things like operating agreements, lease agreements, loan documentation, contracts, tax returns, KPIs, pro formas, Profit & Loss Statements, and balance sheets will help speed the due diligence process along. If you cannot or do not comply with buyer requests quickly, the buyers can attempt to wear you down as you drag your feet. Essentially, the buyers can use your inefficiency to pay less for your business.

Yes, due diligence will take some time but if you have been preparing for it, you should know what most buyers will want. Believe it or not, buyers WILL find the things you don't want them to find, so be prepared for it. In fact, if you want to nip it in the bud, go ahead and give the buyers information about the skeletons in your closet. It's okay because they'll find out anyway.

2. **Make due diligence part of a planned exit process.**

If you make the due diligence event part of your business exit process, you can set guidelines. You can require buyers to provide you with all their requests at one time rather than in piecemeal format. Again, buyers are trying to wear you down to get a lower purchase price. If they can make you take time away from operating your business over and over by asking for miniscule things, they can gain a psychological advantage over you.

By setting parameters from the beginning, your team can help you set timelines and limits to the number of buyer requests and on your responses to the requests. Although buyers' teams may kick back a bit, I have found that if you schedule out the events within the due diligence procedures, the process moves along quickly and doesn't tend to get bogged down.

3. **Provide a table of contents for your documents.**

Since you are trying to provide all necessary documents at one time, you want to include a table of contents at the top of your set of pages. This will hold you accountable for what is included in your paperwork, and it will prevent buyers from claiming they didn't receive a report. Potentially, this simple step could save you hours of time and thousands of dollars in legal fees to reorganize and resend documents.

4. **Fight for your "ugly baby."**

I heard someone say years ago that "You should never tell a woman her baby is ugly. If you do, prepare to run because Mama's gonna smack you down." Well, your business is your baby, and you will become a mad mama when someone attacks your business. How dare the buyers say your business isn't operating at peak efficiency or your team isn't doing things they should be doing. You get the picture.

As part of the due diligence process, buyers are going to point out your ugly baby. Your business is going to be fully exposed so go ahead and get ready for it. Buyers will point out all the weaknesses in your business. Then, they will dwell on those weaknesses to convince you that your business is not worth the millions of dollars they offered you in their Letter of Intent.

5. **Don't forget the big picture.**

Many times, the due diligence process can drag on for months and months. You will probably get frustrated. I've been there. I know how frustrating and stressful it can be. This process can stir up all kinds of emotions, and truthfully, some buyers hope to get you all worked up. If you are emotionally weary or frustrated, they believe they can sway your resolve.

As the old saying goes, now is when you must "kill them with kindness." You have to remember that the buyers' goal in the due diligence process is to expose the ugliness of your business to validate a reduction in the purchase price. However, you want to be kind while you remain firm fighting for your ugly baby.

Your kindness might catch buyers off guard and convince them that *you* are worth the original purchase price even if your business has flaws. If you can maintain a clear head and a kind heart during this sometimes ugly process, buyers might be more likely to give you the benefit of the doubt or be kinder in their own assertions about your company.

6. **Do you own due diligence on the buyer.**

If there is an earnout, buyout, or seller-carried note within the purchase agreement, now is the time you want to conduct your own due diligence, almost like countersurveillance. In this case, though, you'll need to tell the buyers exactly what you are going to do. You will be relying on them to provide your earnout, your buyout, your seller-carried note, or your salaried contract. Therefore, you have permission to ask for the buyers' payment history. Maybe you ask for permission to run a credit report or a background check. In my opinion, what's "good for the goose is good for the gander."

To me, due diligence is a tedious, stressful process, so I have provided you with several steps that can help reduce everyone's stress. So go ahead and let buyers bring in their inspectors. Have them throw the baby's car seat down the hill, if you will. It will be okay. If buyers want to see the business four times before the closing date, let them.

Part of the due diligence process is full exposure. If you are aware of that when you begin, you can cope with any repairs that are needed or price adjustments that are made.

Obviously, there are many more due diligence survival techniques than the ones I listed but the ones I gave you provide a high-level view of the process. If you find yourself in this phase, enjoy it. It can be tons of fun if you know how to play the game.

CHAPTER 40

TIE UP LOOSE ENDS

"It is the loose ends with which men hang themselves."
Zelda Fitzgerald

Once buyers uncover information about your business from the due diligence process, they may ask for allowances or changes to be made to the formal sales agreement, also known as the purchase agreement. The closing of your business sale hinges upon the acceptance of that purchase agreement by both buying and selling agents, so you must stay diligent and tie up any loose ends from the negotiation period within this document.

NEFARIOUS SELLER?

When I was 18 years old, I purchased my first business, a small landscaping company. Since the purchase price was relatively low, I thought I could close the deal without having a lawyer review it. Yeah, rookie mistake. I know. At the time, though, the legal costs seemed insurmountable compared to the low purchase price.

Fast forward some 18 months after I purchased the company. I received a letter from the state of Georgia letting me know that the previous owner had not paid the last portion of the unemployment taxes, and I was now the person responsible. Clearly, I didn't have good counsel when I bought the company, but the seller did, and his attorney made sure that he was protected in the event we had overlooked something. And we did.

The seller was not trying to be nefarious. He just had a good lawyer who used the purchase agreement to protect his client from future liabilities or claims against his company or him.

USE THE PURCHASE AGREEMENT TO RESOLVE OR ACCOUNT FOR PRESENT ISSUES

Maybe you have overlooked a tax or insurance liability. Perhaps you have forgotten a personal guarantee you made on a lease agreement. Due to confusion during the closing process, maybe you didn't realize you owed one more month of expenses to a vendor, or perhaps an employee has filed a harassment suit against one of your business managers. Whatever your particular "loose ends are," you want to use the purchase agreement to tie them up.

When your team is drafting up terms and conditions within the purchase agreement, you will need to build a list of liabilities that could come back to bite you after closing the sale. Now don't worry; if you have a powerhouse exit team, they will help you. They can ask you directed questions to identify any recurring, existing, or upcoming problems in your company. In the meantime, you need to go ahead and dig through the closets to see if there are any skeletons in there.

In particular, you should answer the following questions to know which loose ends need to be tied up in the sales agreement:

- What agreements have you signed that are still in force?

- Have you made agreements with outside consultants?

- Are you carrying loans on a piece of equipment?

- Did you make any personal guarantees with landlords, vendors, or advertisers?

- Do you have any looming liabilities (angry customers, disgruntled former employees, product failures, lawsuits) that could cause you problems?

- Who owns copyrights to your logo?

- Do you have current contracts on your management systems or websites?

WAYS A PURCHASE AGREEMENT PROTECTS THE SELLER

I realize this is not the happiest topic and can even be called depressing, but you want to dig up ALL the skeletons. In your meetings with your exit team, be transparent. Get everything out and on the table so that your team can help you. NOW is the time for you to take inventory and take action. If you wait until after the sale, your team cannot protect you. However, before the sale, your legal team can add releases, clauses, and requirements to the purchase agreement which can shield you from known and unknown liabilities after the sale. Specifically, your attorney can add one or all of the following terms and conditions within the purchase agreement:

- A Release

  Just what it sounds like, this clause releases the seller from specific and/or general liabilities or obligations that could arise after the sale. The more specific the release, the better protected you become.

- An Indemnification Clause

  Also called a Hold Harmless Clause, this condition protects the seller from any lawsuits that arise after the sale. I like the way Anna Wang of ShakeLaw.com defines this clause. She explains, "An indemnity clause typically states that one party agrees to 'indemnify' (and often also to 'hold harmless' and 'defend') the other party. To indemnify someone is to absorb the losses caused by that party, rather than seeking compensation from that party, or to compensate that party if something you do (or fail to do) causes them to experience loss, damages, or a lawsuit from a third party."[50]

- Insurance

  If the seller's skeletons require releases or indemnifications, attorneys might require buyers to purchase and carry liability insurance to cover potential obligations if they should arise. That way, if a situation comes up, the insurance company could deal with the legal and financial ramifications.

WAYS A PURCHASE AGREEMENT PROTECTS THE BUYER

While the release, indemnification, and insurance help provide you with some peace of mind, buyers might ask you to sign certain agreements that could come back to haunt you. If you sign these agreements without reading through them, you could strip away all the protections you just put in place in the terms and conditions, so look out for these common agreements in the purchase agreement. Have your exit team review them and write in conditions that protect you before you sign:

- Non-Compete Agreement

  In the case of a business sale, you are going to have to sign this agreement. A buyer usually enforces it to prevent you from going to work for a competitor's company or from opening a new competing business. If buyers are purchasing your trade secrets, patents, formulas, and the like, they have the right to ask you to leave that information in their hands and no one else's, at least for a certain amount of time.

  However, you will want to rely on your team to add protective terms and conditions to the purchase agreement. While you cannot work for

---

50 Wang, Anna. May 2014. Indemnity Clauses: Understanding the Basics. Retrieved from http://www.shakelaw.com/blog/indemnity-clauses-understanding-basics/

competitors, make sure you maintain the right to work with businesses who do not compete.

Also, make sure you specify a realistic time limit around the non-compete. Typically, 12, 18, 24, or 36 months allow buyers to make the company their own so that if you decide to compete, they can withstand your competition.

Lastly, you want to make sure the non-compete terminates in the event of a breach of contract. If the buyers do not pay their obligations to you, stipulate the dissolution of the agreement so that you can attempt to take back their customers and the industry niche if you so choose.

- Non-Solicit Agreement

Most likely, you are also going to have to sign a non-solicit agreement. Once again, this document governs you. Essentially, it prevents you from poaching current employees, customers, and vendors from the company once you sell it.

If you want to operate a non-competing business after the sale, you may have your attorney include certain conditions within this agreement. For instance, you may request the right to hire employees if the buyers fire them, or if you want to take employees with you, stipulate that within this agreement so the buyers know about it and agree to it. Just remember, if you take key employees with you, the buyers have the right to lower their purchase price for your company.

- Indemnification Agreement

I mentioned indemnification clauses that protect you, but in this part of an indemnification agreement, buyers will ask for protection for them. By signing this agreement, you indemnify the buyers if someone claims that you did something wrong while operating the company.

Obviously, it's fair to protect the buyers from any illegal activity done during your tenure in the business, like fraud, tax evasion, or infringement. However, you should not have to indemnify the buyers for everyday, legal operating procedures that were done during your ownership of the business. Again, your attorney will be able to help determine what is fair and what is not.

- Confidentiality Agreement

Basically, you and the buyers agree to keep your secrets secret in the agreement. The buyers have already asked you not to compete with them but now they have the right to ask you to keep your trade secrets from competitors as well.

Confidentiality agreements are standard but make sure you maintain the right to speak with your legal and financial teams about how you are getting compensated for the sale of your business. Keep your trade secrets secret but use common sense when you define other terms within the confidentiality agreement.

- Intellectual Property Agreement

Another agreement that you may have to sign is the Intellectual Property Agreement. If you have patents, copyrights, or trademarks on products or systems within your company, you agree to give the buyers rights to use them. You are not giving away your intellectual property. Rather, you are giving the buyers permission to use it.

If you worked with an outside consultant on that patent or design, buyers will need that third party to sign this agreement as well. All parties who created the property must give the buyers permission to use it, or buyers have the right to walk away from the deal or lower their offer price.

Whew. You already have many documents to review, and I haven't even given you an exhaustive list of terms, conditions, gotchas, etc., within the purchase agreement. I just hit some highlights! Then, how do you identify potentially harmful clauses as you read through the dozens or hundreds of pages within the agreement? How do you protect yourself while allowing the buyer to protect himself?

- Listen to your advisors.

  You pay your team to think about worst-case scenarios. They are here to protect you from financial and emotional harm, and they are familiar with the legal terminology in purchase agreements. Listen to what they say because they know what they're doing.

- Take inventory.

  No one knows your business better than you do currently. You know what skeletons you have buried, so write down everything you can think of that could come back to haunt you. Then, let your advisors determine the risk those skeletons could pose to your or the buyer.

- Prepare to negotiate the details.

  There will be some give and take through the negotiations over the terms and conditions within the purchase agreement. If you know your business has problems, be prepared to negotiate. Don't give in to all of the buyers' demands because your business has some ugly spots. Get creative, and let your team help you negotiate.

- Do not forget about the team you are leaving behind.

  More than likely, you have employees that will remain with the company. They will be exposed to liabilities if they exist, so put conditions in place that will take care of your former team.

The clauses and agreements within a purchase agreement tie up business loose ends before the sale of the company, and they protect you and buyers from legal and financial retribution after the sale of the company. Now that you know how a sales agreement can protect and hurt you, let's look at the general information and sections included within one.

CHAPTER 41

DRAW UP A PURCHASE AGREEMENT

"Your life works to the degree you keep your agreements."
Werner Erhard

N ow that you know to include certain protective terms and conditions in the purchase agreement, you need to know where to put them. While the document does indeed protect buyers and sellers, it does so much more than that, too. Essentially, the purchase agreement outlines and answers everything about the business sale.

RELY ON YOUR TEAM, BUT READ FOR YOURSELF

On a Friday evening around 7:00, I was walking down the beach in South Georgia when my email chimed. It was here...the draft of the purchase agreement for my company. As I began scrolling through the document on my Blackberry, I had two specific thoughts. First, I thought, "Holy Batman! This thing is crazy long. I mean, it's book length!" The second was, "I'm so glad I have a superstar attorney who can review this thing in detail and tell me what in the world it all means."

I have seen many, many business purchase agreements over the years as a CFP®, as a CEPA, and as a business owner. Yet, I am still surprised and amazed at the length of these documents. The longer I'm in business, the longer these documents seem to get. A final business purchase agreement will likely include 10 to 20 different types of agreements, from employment agreements to non-solicit agreements to consulting agreements. Easily, the final stack of documents could include 200 to 300 or more pages of legal jargon. That will make you want to give up pizza; it's that depressing.

I remember the first business purchase agreement I held in my hands. Like any seller, I took out a highlighter and commenced to reading every line. After about 15 minutes, I surveyed my markings only to notice that just about every page had a note or a question. Laughing to myself, I realized that I didn't need to know everything in the document; I hired people to do that. It is their job to make sure I am protected.

However, I do want to understand what I'm signing. I don't want to be so worn down by the due diligence and sales process that I sign whatever is placed in front of me. After all, if I go to court over something related to my business or its sale, the attorney on the opposing side will say, "Mr. Goodbread, did you ever read this document before you signed it?" If I have not read it, nothing I say matters after I say, "No" or "Not thoroughly."

Yes, you will rely on your attorney to handle most of the terms and conditions, but you need a cursory knowledge of what should be or could be in the business purchase agreement. That way, you can review it for mistakes and gain a thorough understanding of it before you get to the closing table. In no particular order, I will provide you with a list of sections that can be included in the business purchase agreement. Some lawyers will combine the sections I list, or they will include information I have put in one section in a different section, but each segment of the sales agreement explains the who, what, when, where, how, and how much of the business sale.

DESCRIPTION OF THE PARTIES

Appearing at the beginning of the document, this section provides the following information about buyers and sellers:

- Legal names
- Addresses
- Phone numbers

DESCRIPTION OF BUSINESS

Also known as the Sellers' Representations and Warranties, this section provides a detailed description of the following things:

- Location of the business
- Purpose of the business
- Services the business provides
- Products the company sells
- Business entity under which the company operates
- Management structure of the business
- Management systems the business uses
- Past, present, and future financials
- Types of customers who come into the business or who use the business's services

DESCRIPTION OF SALE

Absolutely vital to the purchase agreement, this section identifies the following:

- Type of sale (asset, stock, earnout, seller-carried note, and/or seller employment)
- Description of every asset, stock, and item included in the sale
- Description of every asset, stock, and item excluded from the sale

TRANSFER OF PROPERTY

Hinging upon the description of sellable assets, stocks, and items, this section can include the following:

- Seller's Agreement to Sell the listed assets, stocks, and items
- Buyer's Agreement to Purchase the listed assets, stocks, and items

PURCHASE PRICE

Once the document identifies what is and is not included in the business sale, the purchase agreement will outline the following:

- Price buyers are paying for the listed assets, items, and/or stocks
- How the buyer plans to pay for the business (can include outside financing, seller-carried notes, seller employment, and/or stock buyouts)

ASSUMPTION OF RISK AND LIABILITIES (SOMETIMES ONE-AND-THE-SAME AS COVENANT)

This section often dictates which party assumes responsibility for the following risks and liabilities before and after closing:

- Product loss
- Loss of revenue
- Tax liabilities
- Third-party fees
- Loan obligations
- Vendor obligations
- Employee salaries

COVENANTS (OFTEN SPLIT INTO BUYER AGREEMENTS AND SELLER AGREEMENTS)

If separated from the Assumption of Risk section, many of the protective clauses I discussed in the previous chapter can appear in this section. Look for any:

- Indemnification Agreements
- Business Conduct Agreements
- Non-Compete Agreements
- Non-Solicit Agreements

- Confidentiality Agreements
- Intellectual Property Agreements

TRANSITION

So that no party runs away from responsibility after the closing, many lawyers will include this section to:

- Clarify the seller's role within the business after the sale.
- Determine who will teach and train the new owners and any new employees.
- Specify who will notify vendors and customers that the business has transferred ownership.

PARTICIPATION OR ABSENCE OF BROKERS

If buyers and/or sellers have engaged a third-party facilitator during the sale process, the business purchase agreement will:

- List legal names, titles, and addresses of any third-party facilitators involved in the business's sale.
- Stipulate which party pays the facilitator's fees, what the facilitator did to earn his wages, and how much compensation he will receive upon the business's closing.

CONDITIONS

One of the easier-to-understand sections of the purchase agreement, this section:

- Provides a location for the closing.
- Lists the time closing will occur.
- Issues title transfers.
- Specifies what monies will be delivered (paid) upon closing.

MISCELLANEOUS

While many sellers believe "miscellaneous" means "not important," that is far from the truth. This section can:

- Reveal purchase price allocations.
- Adjust purchase price to reflect prorated business expenses, inventory, or accounts receivable on closing day.
- Outline how to resolve party disputes if they occur.

SIGNATURES

Appearing at the end of the document, the buyers and sellers will sign their agreement to the terms and conditions outlined in the document. A representative attorney, banker, broker, or CEPA in attendance at the closing will also sign as a witness and notarize the buyer and seller signatures.

EXHIBITS/APPENDICES

Attached to the purchase agreements, any of these documents can be included in this section:

- Financial statements and reports
- The Letter of Intent
- Signed agreements
- Leasehold agreements/transfers
- Vendor agreements/transfers
- Asset valuations
- Owner and/or employee biographies
- Industry reports
- Marketing plans and contracts

ASSIGN ROLES TO YOUR TEAM MEMBERS

Whew! I didn't even list all the sections that can be included in a purchase agreement, and I'm tired!

After you do your own review, you'll want to gain insights from your exit team. Everyone—your attorney, your transition specialist, your CPA, your CEPA, and your CFP®—will need to be on the same page, but while you will need input from each member, you need to designate one person to act as the play caller here to prevent head-butting, frustration, and stagnation.

In my experience, the attorney is best suited to facilitate any changes needed and to make the final call on terms and conditions within the purchase agreement but if you are working with a sharp attorney, she should not have any ego issues. Instead she will listen respectfully to insight from all the other professionals. With that said, you also need to task another exit team member to play quarterback and keep the ball moving down the field. Just as I usually ask an attorney to step into the coach's role here, I normally ask the CEPA to fill this position. Oftentimes, this team member has the knowledge necessary to prevent continuances and keep other team members (buyers and sellers) on task and on schedule.

CHAPTER 42

CIRCUMVENT A RETRADE

*"There is no chance, no destiny, no fate that can circumvent
or hinder or control the firm resolve of a determined soul."*

Ella Wheeler Wilcox

A s your team members are finalizing the purchase agreement, you are getting ready for "payday." What happens, though, when you get a call from one of your exit team members who tells you that the buyer has asked for a last-minute price reduction…a retrade? Hearing those words will either have you wondering what is going on or spiraling into a whirlwind of anxiety. Whichever person you are, you need to understand why retrades occur in a business sale so that you can see if there is anything you can do in advance to avoid hearing that dreaded word.

RETRADE DEFINED

Steven Sneiderman – law partner, CEPA®, member of the Exit Planning Institute's Chapter Leadership Team, and Mergers & Acquisitions expert – describes a retrade as "an unanticipated adverse modification to the previously agreed to terms and conditions of a transaction, most frequently in the purchase price."[51] An unanticipated adverse modification sounds pretty bad, doesn't it? But what does it mean? In my *financially simple* terms, a retrade is a

---

51 Sneiderman, Steven H. February 2013. What's a retrade, and how do I prevent one?
   Retrieved from http://www.crainscleveland.com/article/20130206/BLOGS05/130209898/
   whats-a-retrade-and-how-do-i-prevent-one

renegotiation of the purchase agreement which usually means that the purchase price is going down.

Currently, retrade in a business sale is most common in the business broker's world. Frankly, because M&A Advisors and investment bankers usually perform a higher level of due diligence, have more team members at their disposal, and have better technological systems available to them than business brokers typically do, their business sales do not undergo retrades as often as those of the business broker. However, retrades can and do still occur under each facilitator's guidance.

WHY RETRADES OCCUR

Oftentimes, a retrade happens when the due diligence process reveals something unexpected about your company that poses a risk for the buyers, costs them money, or simply makes them uncomfortable.

Possibly, the buyers unearthed skeletons that may or will affect the company after the closing date. What if a terminated employee has threatened to file a lawsuit? Assuming the buyers still want to purchase the company, they will probably lower their offer to assume that risk. They will have to purchase extra liability insurance, and they might have to spend time and money on a legal battle. Therefore, they will offer less for your business.

Sometimes during a lengthy due diligence process, your business's performance will suffer, and its profitability will wane. Other times, the buyers could realize that you inflated your future performance predictions when financial reports provided at the end of the due diligence process do not match the profitable prediction of the pro forma you gave the sellers at the beginning of the process. In those instances, the buyers will probably lower their offer.

What if your landlord will not honor your building rental agreement for the buyers? After purchasing the business, the buyers may have to find new retail space and move equipment, assets, and inventory. Costs to do that add up, and the buyers may request a lower purchase price to cover those expenses.

Unexpected circumstances often occur during business sale negotiations, and the buyer lowers the purchase price for legitimate reasons. However, some buyers plan to retrade since they delivered their Letter of Intent to purchase your business.

I've seen buyers lock up sellers in a Letter of Intent and then drag their feet *intentionally* during the due diligence process. Thinking the business is as good as sold, buyers relax their marketing or selling, but then the company doesn't perform as expected and here come the buyers demanding a retrade. I consider this instance an intentional bait and switch.

Another type of bait and switch I've seen buyers use is the strong-handed retrade. Some buyers intentionally drag out the discovery process, or the due diligence process, to outlast any other interested buyers. By the time due diligence ends, the buyers lower the purchase price knowing that the seller is exhausted and has no buyers still interested in the company.

CIRCUMVENT A RETRADE

No matter why a retrade occurs, the word can cause nightmares for business owners, so how can you avoid this reduction in the purchase price?

- Prepare your company.

  This point seems obvious but as I've mentioned many times before, you must prepare for the future. If you have prepared your company correctly, you will have a close-to-accurate idea of your company's value before you enter the due diligence process.

- Keep your projections as conservative as possible.

  Don't set the value of your company too low when you offer it for sale but don't inflate its value either. I worked with one client who inflated her company's financial projections on her pro forma against her exit team's advice. Ultimately, the buyer dragged out the due diligence process to see if her projections could come to fruition. When they did not, he lowered his purchase offer significantly. If the client had been more honest, more prepared, and more conservative in her projections, she might have prevented the retrade.

- Be ready to walk away from the table.

  While this option is risky like a game of roulette, it can be extremely effective. So many times, I've seen sellers so eager to sell they forget that they can walk away if they must. Some sellers cannot walk away; I get that. However, some have the power to walk away or threaten to walk away if buyers lower the purchase price. Although threatening to walk can prevent a retrade, it can also dissolve the business sale, so if you threaten to walk, be prepared to walk away.

- Check out the buyer before you enter into the agreement.

  Like I mentioned in Chapter 39, do some due diligence on the buyers. What are their histories? Is retrading a standard operating procedure for them? Do they make high offers for businesses, drag out the discovery process, and then offer far less in a retrade? Are the buyers approved for financing, or do they still need approval for financing? Use this due diligence time to determine the buyers' suitability.

- Never procrastinate.

  When the seller can provide the buyers with requested (and accurate) information in a prompt manner, buyers often view the seller as a strong, confident, prepared candidate. If you consistently provide information in a timely manner, it can build confidence on the buyers' side that your company is worth what you are asking for it.

  Additionally, if you know you have skeletons in your company's closet, preemptively identify them. Only then can your exit team help you prepare for the fallout that might occur. If your team and the buyers know the "sordid" details from the beginning, then teams can set an appropriate purchase price to prevent a retrade.

- Do not try to sell in a bad market.

  A CPA friend of mine recently told me that "if real estate is about location, location, location, then the business sale is about timing,

timing, timing." In some ways, I think he's correct. Trying to sell a business in a bad market usually doesn't work. In a bad market, you are likely to set yourself up for a retrade, so use common sense here.

CALL A BUYER'S BLUFF

If you are working with buyers who say, "I'm lowering the price of my offer," what do you do? How do you tell if they are bluffing or strong-arming you? Like I said, some buyers are practicing the bait and switch method. How do you tell if this is what your buyers are doing?

Well, most simply, see if their actions match their words. Are they "playing hard to get" or playing with your emotions? Maybe they're saying they are not interested anymore but they are still hanging around your company. They're still asking your employees questions and calling to check on your business. They're still "around." Sure, they may say, "Take this offer or leave it," but they are hovering. That can indicate that their new offer is a bluff to see if they can get you to lower your purchase price.

Now, I will say this. If you or your team call the buyers and get no response, that is their response. If you said no to the retrade and then the buyers do not accept any more correspondence from you, they are gone. They weren't bluffing so be sure buyers are bluffing before you say "No" to the retrade.

Retrades can be frustrating, especially this late in the selling process of your business. They don't have to be, though. You can prepare yourself long before you get to that point. You can take certain actions to avoid a retrade or to prevent it from happening. If you find yourself in a retrade situation, though, you still have options to protect yourself and minimize the damage.

CHAPTER 43

PREVENT BACKOUTS

"Not all change and disruption succeeds, to be sure."
Kristen Soltis Anderson

Not only must you prepare for a retrade as negotiations over purchase price and purchase agreement terms and conditions draw to a close, you must also anticipate other last-minute changes. Even if you are ready to sign on the dotted line, plans could change, and while some changes can be good, most changes before the sale of your business negatively affect the closing of your business sale. Changes usually mean that the buyers have changed their minds, so let's look at common reasons a buyer backs out of the sale of a business. Then, let's figure out how to handle those disruptions.

LAST MINUTE CHANGES CAN BE BAD

Perhaps one of the saddest last-minute changes I've read about transpired around the sinking of the Titanic. Right before the ship left its harbor, Second Officer David Blair was removed from the crew. Depending on which source you read, he may have taken a key to a locker that contained binoculars for the lookout, or he may have forgotten to tell others where he left the key to the box. No matter what happened, sources tend to agree that lookouts on the Titanic were not using binoculars the night the ship hit the iceberg.

If the lookouts used binoculars that night, could they have prevented the boat's crash? Who knows. Regardless, a last-minute disruption to the Titanic's crew staffing caused confusion. That confusion led to disruptions in standard operating procedures. Those disruptions may or may not have prevented the sinking of the Titanic.

LAST MINUTE CHANGES CAN BE GOOD

Sometime, though, last minute changes can be good. On August 28, 1963, Martin Luther King, Jr. (one of my heroes) delivered a speech in front of the Lincoln Memorial during the March on Washington at the height of the Civil Rights Movement. Sources say that when Dr. King was nearing the end of his speech, audience member and friend, Mahalia Jackson, shouted out, "Tell 'em about 'The Dream,' Martin!"[52]

From that point on, Dr. King began to improvise and speak from his heart instead of from his prepared notes. Because of this unexpected disruption, Dr. King went on to deliver what some call "one of the most iconic speeches in American history" that became "one of the defining moments of the Civil Rights Movement."[53]

COMMON REASONS A BUYER BACKS OUT OF PURCHASING A BUSINESS

With these life-changing disruptions as our backdrop, I want to talk to you about changes that can occur before the closing of your business sale. Though some positive changes can occur (i.e. buyers raise their offer), most changes that happen right before the sale cause disruptions, so let's look at four types of disruptions that can prevent the closing of a business sale:

1. **Financing Falls Apart**

    Just like in real estate, buyers' financing can fall apart. I have worked on many business sales where buyers had written approval from the bank. I've helped put deals together based on the buyers' Letter of

52 History. (n.d.) 'I Have a Dream' Speech. Retrieved from https://www.history.com/topics/i-have-a-dream-speech
53 Tikkanen, Amy. (n.d.). I Have a Dream: Speech by King [1963]. Retrieved from https://www.britannica.com/topic/I-Have-A-Dream

Intent and approval from the lender. Everything has been ready to go. Then, one small contingency in a lender's underwriting changes everything.

Maybe the bank requires more or updated documentation. Parties can provide the necessary items, but they must delay the closing until the underwriter reviews and approves the new information, or worse, the lender might refuse to issue the final approval and release funds on the buyers' loan because something didn't meet their "sniff test." If the buyers can't get financing, they cannot purchase the business.

2. **Parties Become Disgruntled**

Sometimes, buyers have nothing to do with the disruption of the business sale. While you might think disagreements arise most often between buyers and sellers, that has not been my experience. More often, I've seen business sales dissolve over disagreements between partners, members, or shareholders.

If you are on the seller's side and you have partners or shareholders, you must make sure each is working toward the same end goal. Let's say that one of the partners has his own selling agenda or wants a different sales outcome. Then, sellers could end up on different pages at the end of the process. If co-sellers cannot reach their own internal agreements, they cannot move forward with a purchase agreement with the buyer.

3. **Third Parties Cause Delays**

I've also seen disruptions arise due to parties unaffiliated with either buyers or sellers. Perhaps you must delay closing because you are waiting on a landlord to validate and approve the new leasees (the buyers), or maybe a supplier or vendor refuses to transfer a contract from seller to buyer. Many times, situations outside of buyers' and sellers' immediate control delay or disrupt closings.

4. The Deal Dies

Worst of all, the deal could just die. Some buyers get right up to the purchasing table and get cold feet. I've even seen some sellers get cold feet and walk away from the closing. One seller I knew decided he didn't like the buyer, and he walked away from the sale during the due diligence process.

Many times, sellers are locked into the deal and cannot walk away. Legal documents and agreements bind them to the sale. However, buyers, at times, have the ability to walk away for one reason or the other. I've even seen a buyer walk away from the business sale because he was diagnosed with a terminal illness after he issued his Letter of Intent.

DISASTER HAPPENED; WHAT CAN I DO NOW?

You never know what could happen before the business sale closes, so what are you to do when you find yourself facing unexpected disruptions?

- Reduce the purchase price - The most common thing sellers do to keep the deal moving forward is reduce the purchase price. Sometimes, bank underwriters will require sellers to lower the sales price to approve funds for the buyers. Other times, buyers will demand recompense for major issues uncovered within the business during the due diligence process. To proceed with the sale, the seller will lower the purchase price as compensation.

- Place a guarantee on the sale - Sometimes, a seller is waiting on a major contract to fund or significant accounts receivable to come in. Many times, a seller will have to reduce the purchase price or add a seller guarantee to the deal to get to the closing table. Thus, if sales do not hit the target everyone expects, then the seller guarantees a reduction in purchase price or a payback to the buyer later.

- Put a holdback in place - In a holdback, parties take a portion of the purchase price and put it in an escrow account. If the company does not receive anticipated funds, then the money goes back to the buyers, thus reducing the purchase price. However, if the company does receive the funds, the money is released to the seller.

- Offer an earnout - As discussed in Chapter 32, this option allows buyers to give the seller a fair market price for the company upon closing, but it provides a bonus or profit percentage to the seller if the business does well over a set amount of time. Thus, if you believe your company is worth more than the buyers are willing to give, both parties can get to the closing table.

The key here is that you must remember that unexpected roadblocks do not always mean the deal is dead. Disruptions don't always mean you have to go backward and start from scratch on a deal with different buyers. Oftentimes, there are still ways to get the deal done and sell the business. However, if you can plan your exit well enough in advance, you can virtually eliminate some or most disruptions. With the technology available today, you should be able to avoid most surprises, but sometimes things happen that are outside of your control, so you must plan how to deal with those circumstances as well.

CLOSE THE SALE

"It always seems impossible until it's done."
Nelson Mandela

Both buyer and seller have now reached agreements, and negotiations are over. You've reached the actual sale of your business!

CHAPTER 44

CLOSE THE DEAL

*"Look, don't congratulate us when we buy a company,
congratulate us when we sell it. Because any fool can overpay
and buy a company, as long as money will last to buy it."*

Henry Kravis

J ust about every fall, the United States enters final rounds of an election season. Candidates have been travelling around, voicing their platforms for months and maybe years, and as candidates race for a voter's final nod, the election process can get quite ugly. If you watch any election coverage (past or present), you are bound to see candidates or candidate representatives calling each other names, bashing each other's agendas, or even throwing actual punches.

With that extreme picture in mind, let's talk about what will actually happen at the closing table when you sell your business. We have spent an entire book talking about selling your business, so let's sell it!

LOCATION

Many times in today's advancing technological world, closings will take place virtually via audio or video conferencing. Lawyers will have both parties use electronic signature software, or they will have the parties sign paperwork and send the original documents via overnight mail delivery. For sellers and buyers who live in different locales, this option can save travel time, and for those people whose schedules pull them 100 different directions a day, the virtual close can save them time away from other responsibilities.

However, some buyers and sellers don't like the impersonal feel of the virtual closing. I've even heard clients call them "cold" and "anticlimactic." After all the work buyers and sellers have done to get to the closing table, many want a more formal, nostalgic type of closing. Typically, these live-paper closings take place at the buyer's attorney's office.

THE MAIN EVENT

While virtual closings are fairly straightforward and predictable, live-paper closings leave room for creative celebratory activities. Sure, I've been in my fair share of boring closings where people sit around a table, sharing platitudes and getting down to the business at hand, but I've also been at live-paper closings with fancy buffets, photographers, 3' x 5' representative cardboard checks, and expensive gifts for all who attend.

No matter how or where buyers and sellers meet to sign on the dotted line, there is no doubt that all will sign, and sign, and sign, and sign. It's inevitable. You see, all the documents we have covered are now in final print. You are at the closing table to place your signature or initials in blue ink on *every page* of the purchase agreement. Even if some documents do not include signatory blank lines, most attorneys will still have you sign or initial the right-hand corners of every page. This proves that you have reviewed and agreed to each, and since the purchase agreement could include 200-300 pages of documents, you'll be signing, and signing, and signing, so be prepared for that.

Additionally, since all those pages must be notarized, don't forget to carry a copy of your driver's license with you. Don't be like a client of mine who showed up to closing without his wallet and delayed closing until someone from his office could bring it. Don't be "that guy."

FUNDING

After you sign all the documents, be prepared to leave the table *without* a check. Yep, you heard me correctly. More than likely, you are not going to get a check for selling your business that day. Now, I have seen several legal teams go in and make those huge, 3' x 5' prize-winning checks and have the parties pose with them for posterity's sake, but more than likely, you are not going to receive the money after signing the paperwork.

You see, the buyers' attorney has to confirm things like title changes and contract transfers. Many small transactions must be funded before you receive your final payment, too. In fact, some of the people around the table (like your business broker, your attorney, your CEPA, etc.) may receive a check at the time of closing, even though you do not, and that can be frustrating to many people.

THE AFTER PARTY

After the formalities of document signings at the closing table, the business broker or M&A Advisor will often arrange and sometimes pay for a celebratory dinner. If your exit team sets up a dinner, they will usually schedule closing in the late afternoon so that everyone can leave the closing table and go directly to a nice dinner. I've been to many of these celebrations where exit team members, employee team members, friends, and family members attend.

Many times, these events are not that dissimilar to a wedding celebration except you are the best man, and the bride is your business. Most likely, you'll get up and give a speech. Maybe you'll tell funny stories about highs and lows you experienced in your business over the years. You will recognize key people who helped you along your way, and you may even have gifts for certain employees, advisors, and others.

YOUR NEXT STEP

I clearly remember my first business sale. I signed the documents, and my wife and I went out with some friends to celebrate the accomplishment. It was not until I got home and laid down for the night that it hit me.... What did I just do? You know, I just sold my business. Did I make the right move? What do I do now? Worries and questions ran through my head all night long, and honestly, that happened to me the two other times I have sold my businesses since then.

You will probably be in the same boat I was. At the end of the day your business sells, you are going to experience a myriad of emotions. Everything for which you have worked has now come to fruition. Your friends, family members, advisors, planners, and employees will probably be there throughout the day to celebrate with you. By the time you get to the end of the day, the adrenaline will wear off. Things will settle down, and anxiety may creep in.

Obviously, you are going to experience excitement and happiness. I mean, you have planned this day for years! However, you will probably second-guess your decision, too, so whenever you reach this point in your business, remember that it is just the start. There is so much more to life! No matter how old or young you are, there is so much more to do! You can volunteer, start another business, travel, spend time with family. You name it, and you can do it!

Ultimately, a closing day does not have to be the end. It can be your new beginning. Although you will experience some sadness and fear, you have permission to rejoice, too! Before you pack up your bags and head out on your adventures, though, we have a few more details to discuss. You must know what to do with your newfound wealth before you go out and spend it!

CHAPTER 45

USE THE MONEY WISELY

"People value and spend their money more wisely
when they acquire it by their own efforts – also known as work."

Larry Elder

You are about to receive a financial windfall; what will you do with the money after the sale of your business? We have now reached the point that I start talking from my CERTIFIED FINANCIAL PLANNER™ point of view. Perhaps you have read through this book and have been wondering when I will start discussing personal financial strategies. Well, I have intentionally delayed talking about money and investments. You see, most folks think financial guys just talk about stocks, bonds, and mutual funds. Sure, I do some of that, but since I specialize in working with business owners, I do so much more than that. So, today is the day. Now is when "Justin the CFP®" talks.

CHANGING THINGS UP

Before I get into the nitty-gritty of what you can do with the proceeds of your business sale, let me say that the information in this chapter **will not** be specific to your individual financial situation. It's designed to give you information and ideas to discuss with your financial professionals. They will be able to advise you according to your investment needs.

I will be discussing financial terms and outlining types of accounts into which business owners can invest, but I don't want you to get so bogged down in financial information that you lose the excitement you have after selling your business. Therefore, if you would like more details about any of these topics, I am including links to articles and videos I have created in the "More Online" section of this book.

WHAT TO DO WITH YOUR FINANCIAL WINDFALL

Many people who win the lottery or receive a large financial windfall end up broke within a few years. You just sold your business. I get that you did not just win the lottery. You have worked your tail off to reach this point, and I realize that. However, like many business owners, you've probably not dealt with this size of cash money before.

Most of your life, you have been dealing with paper net-worth assets listed on your Personal Financial Statement. Yes, you've had this amount of money on paper, but now is the first time you've seen it in your bank account. In the fell-swoops of a pen at the closing table, you've moved your illiquid assets to liquid assets. Reality has struck virtually overnight, and you may feel like you've won the lottery.

If you have been preparing your business for sale over months, years, or a decade, you should be ready for this moment. **You and your financial team should have been working on your personal and business financials long before now**. Hopefully, you and your team have done your personal assessment. You have made plans and investments accordingly, but no matter how much planning you do, your life changes dramatically when you sell your company and receive a mega-payday.

Therefore, let me give you three points that might help you decide what to do with the proceeds from your business sale:

1. **Determine how much income your money needs to earn each year** - Usually done during the exit planning process, this is where you and your financial team calculate how much principal you will use versus how much interest earned off the principal you will use from the proceeds of your business sale.

2. **Build/manage an investment portfolio to meet your determined needs** - Once you know what return you need to earn from the pro-

ceeds of your business sale, you will work with your CFP® to build a tailored investment portfolio. Again, you will usually do this during the exit planning process long before you sell your business.

3. **Practice self-control** - When the proceeds from your sale hit the bank, make sure you follow the investment plan you've put in place, and before the money comes in, make a list of things you will buy or payoff with a portion of the money. That way, you can avoid flaunting your newfound wealth or making unwise emotional purchases. I even tell some of my clients to let their money rest six months before making any purchases over "x" amount of dollars.

INVESTMENT ACCOUNT OPTIONS

The world of investments is extremely complex and difficult to understand. If you are going to invest some of the proceeds from the sale of your business, you need to know where you can put your money. Therefore, I will break things down as simply as possible. By no means is this an all-inclusive list of investment accounts, but it's a good start.

You Can Put Your Money into Qualified Investment Accounts

Qualified accounts are those the government creates for specific purposes and taxes specific ways. Typically, retirement accounts like the following fall into this category:

- IRAs: Traditional or Roth
- SEP IRAs
- 401(k)s
- Self-Employed 401(k)s
- Solo 401(k)s

Some people even consider the following products "qualified accounts" because the government gives them preferred tax treatment:

- Health Savings Accounts (HSAs)
- 529 Savings Plans

You Can Put Your Money into Non-Qualified Investment Accounts

Non-Qualified accounts are those on which the government does not designate purpose or set taxable limitations. They can include the following accounts:

- Individual Checking or Savings Accounts
- Joint Tenant Bank Accounts: Joint Tenants with Rights of Survivorship, Joint Tenants in Common, Joint Tenants in Entirety
- Money Market Accounts
- Business Accounts
- Trust Accounts

ASSETS YOU CAN PURCHASE THROUGH YOUR INVESTMENT ACCOUNTS

Once you have opened one or several types of investment accounts, you can buy assets through those accounts. I will list several common assets in which you could invest, but again, check with your financial advisors for a comprehensive list:

Common Asset Options:

- Stocks
- Bonds
- Certificates of Deposit (CDs)
- Preferred Stocks
- Exchange Traded Funds (ETFs)
- Annuities
- Mutual Funds
- Real Estate

Other Asset Options:

- Master-Limited Partnerships
- Commodities
- Hedge Funds
- Real Estate Investment Trusts (REITs)
- Private Conservatorships
- Personal Collections (Comic Books, Baseball Cards, Gold, etc.)

As I said before, the information I have given you is not specific to your individual situation, so be sure to plan your investments and your retirement goals with your financial professional.

CHAPTER 46

CELEBRATE YOUR ACCOMPLISHMENTS

*"What you get by achieving your goals is not as important
as what you become by achieving those goals."*

Henry David Thoreau

YOU DID IT!

After all of that, I say CONGRATULATIONS! YOU MADE IT! You
sold your business! Job well done! Recalling the statistics from the Exit
Planning Institute, 80 percent of businesses below $50 million in revenue nev-
er sell, so you have just joined an elite minority of business owners. Way to go!

You have just done something that few people have ever done. You have
walked your business to the point where you have made an illiquid asset into
money in the bank. If I could, I would give you a fist bump. Here's a high-five,
too! Boom! Right there! Great job! I'm proud of you.

Go out and celebrate! Have fun but be cautious. Lean on your financial
advisors and family for sound advice and go fulfill your dreams. You have a lot
of living left to do.

Ultimately, I want to say thank you. Thank you for walking through this
Ultimate Sale with me. You make my job worthwhile, and I appreciate you.
Ya'll go out now, and make it a great day!

"Life is hard. Life is fun. Business can be complicated. Money doesn't have to be. Let's continue to make our lives, at least, financially simple."

Justin Goodbread

MORE ONLINE

All the website links mentioned in this book are available for your convenience by visiting FinanciallySimple.com/usale.

WORK WITH JUSTIN...

As an expert in business value growth and exit planning, Justin Goodbread, CFP®, CEPA, CVGA®, is available for:

- One-on-one coaching
- Group coaching
- Exit planning guidance
- Business valuation assessments
- Guest blogging
- Interviews
- Keynote speaking engagements
- Seminars/Workshops/Conferences

Out of respect for Justin's time, we ask that you submit any engagement requests via website form on:

FinanciallySimple.com/work

Justin's team will review your request details and will typically get back to you within 2 business days.

IF YOU WOULD LIKE TO HIRE JUSTIN FOR FINANCIAL ADVICE, INVESTMENT/WEALTH MANAGEMENT, OR BUSINESS PLANNING, PLEASE VISIT THE HERITAGE INVESTORS' WEBSITE.

REMEMBER, LIFE IS GOOD. LIFE IS COMPLICATED, BUT MONEY DOESN'T HAVE TO BE! SO LET'S WORK TOGETHER AND MAKE OUR LIVES, FINANCIALLY SIMPLE!

ACKNOWLEDGEMENTS

First and foremost, I want to thank my lovely bride, Emily. Not only is she the love of my life, she is my biggest supporter and most patient advisor. No matter how far-fetched my goals seem to be or how crazy my shenanigans get, Emily assures me that reaching my goals is entirely possible with God by my side. Emily's encouragement makes me feel like I can conquer the world, and with her by my side, I have accomplished more than I ever thought possible. Honestly, I can't thank her enough for her love and support that makes the world around my insanity, sane. Emily, I love you more than life itself.

Secondly, I want to thank my mother. She and my father invested their lives into mine, and their grand expectations for me have driven me to be the best I can be. Even after my father passed away unexpectedly a couple of years ago, my mother kept pushing me forward to reach my goals, acting as a bulwark in my personal and business life. Thank you, Mom.

Of course, none of this would be remotely possible without my amazing business partner, Jim DeTar. He and I have gone through some extremely tough times together, but no matter how many times I fall, he is there to pick me up and tell me I can get to the end successfully. Undoubtedly, Jim is one of the greatest encouragers in my life.

And lastly, thanks to my Financially Simple™ team for helping me translate my thoughts into a cohesive format, this book and our blog, that will be helping business owners for years to come.

You all have been such an inspiration to me. I would not be here without you!

CPSIA information can be obtained
at www.ICGtesting.com
Printed in the USA
LVHW040050180619
621536LV00003B/4